City & Guilds
Level 1 Certificate for IT Users

Desktop Publishing

Rosemarie Wyatt

Heinemann Educational Publishers
Halley Court, Jordan Hill, Oxford, OX2 8EJ
Part of Harcourt Education

Heinemann is the registered trademark of Harcourt Education Ltd

First published in 2002
2005 2004 2003
10 9 8 7 6 5 4 3 2

A catalogue record for this book is available from the British Library on request.

ISBN 0 435 46264 4

Typeset by Techset Ltd, Gateshead
Printed and bound in Great Britain by Thomson Litho Ltd, Glasgow

Acknowledgements
The screenshots in this book have been reprinted with permission from Microsoft Corporation.

Contents

Introduction

City & Guilds e-Quals is an exciting new range of IT qualifications developed with leading industry experts. These comprehensive, progressive awards cover everything from getting to grips with basic IT to gaining the latest professional skills.

The range consists of both user and practitioner qualifications. User qualifications (Levels 1–3) are ideal for those who use IT as part of their job or in life generally, while Practitioner qualifications (Levels 2–3) have been developed for those who need to boost their professional skills in, for example, networking or software development.

e-Quals boasts on-line testing and a dedicated web site with news and support materials and web-based training. The qualifications reflect industry standards and meet the requirements of the National Qualifications Framework.

With e-Quals you will not only develop your expertise, you will gain a qualification that is recognised by employers all over the world.

Desktop publishing (DTP) software allows you to produce attractive page layouts for documents such as posters and flyers, incorporating images and text in columns. This book assumes the use of Microsoft Publisher 2000 and is for beginners who have a basic knowledge of the mouse and keyboard.

The unit is organised into five outcomes. You will learn to:

- Use the DTP system environment
- Set up given page layouts
- Manipulate text in a DTP file
- Manipulate graphic objects
- Produce printed and file outputs

This book covers the specific skills and underpinning knowledge for the outcomes of the DTP unit although they are not dealt with separately or in the same order.

Each section covers several practical skills as well as underpinning knowledge related to the unit outcomes. This is followed by skills practice and a chance to check your knowledge. Consolidation tasks give you the opportunity to put together skills and knowledge, and practice assignments complete your progress towards the actual assignment. As with all skills, practise makes perfect! Solutions to the skills practice, knowledge checks, consolidation and practice assignments can be found at the back of the book.

There is often more than one way of carrying out a task in Publisher, e.g. using the toolbar, menu or keyboard. Whilst this book may use one method, there are others, and alternatives are listed at the back in the quick reference guide.

The tasks are designed to be worked through in order, as earlier tasks may be used in later sections. Good luck!

Section 1 Getting started

You will learn to

- Load Publisher
- Identify parts of the Publisher window
- Create and set up a new publication
- Create text frames and enter text
- Resize text frames
- Save a publication
- Print a publication
- Close a publication
- Close Publisher
- Close down the computer

In this section you will learn how to load or start up Publisher and to familiarise yourself with the Publisher environment. You will create publications, enter text, save and print.

Information: Using the mouse

The following are terms used to describe mouse actions used in this book:

Click	Press the left mouse button and release.
Double click	Press the left mouse button and release, twice, in quick succession.
Drag	Hold down the left mouse button and drag the mouse to the required position. Release the mouse button.

Task 1.1 Load Publisher

Method

1. Switch on your computer.
2. If you are using a network you will need a user ID and a password to log on. Check with your tutor.
3. Wait for the Windows desktop to appear.

4 Move the mouse pointer over the **Start** button on the taskbar and click the left mouse button – a menu appears (Figure 1.1). Your menus may look slightly different to this depending on the programs available to you.

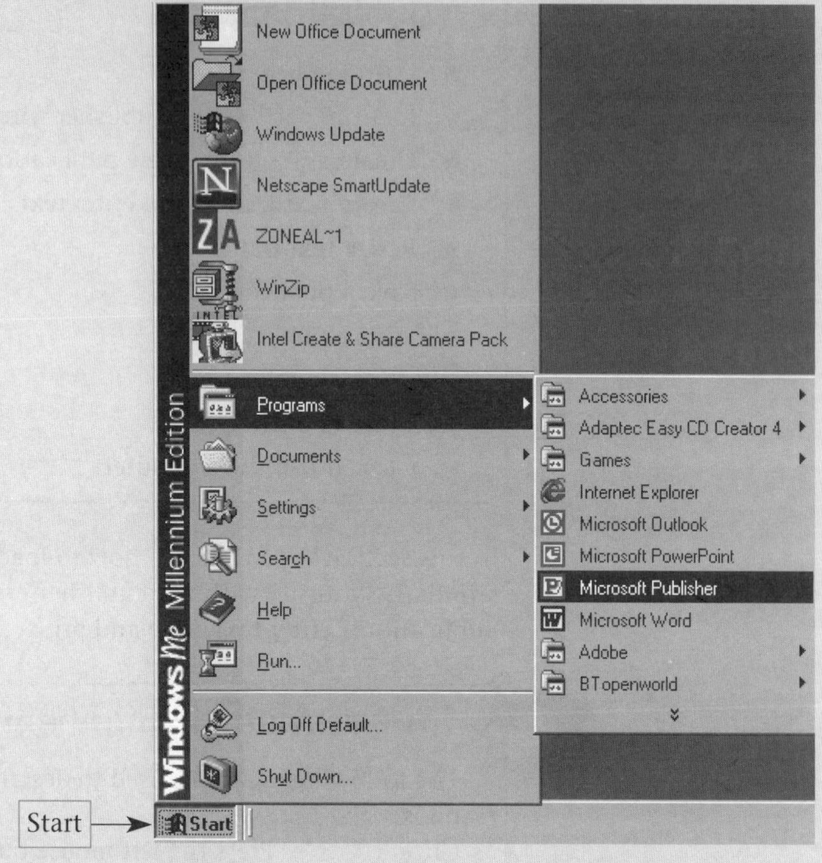

Figure 1.1 Loading Publisher

5 Move the mouse up the menu and point to **Programs** – another menu appears to the right.

6 Move the mouse to **Microsoft Publisher** and click the left button to load. (Depending on your computer's setup, you may have to click on Office 2000 first.)

Alternatively, you may have a Publisher icon on your desktop (Figure 1.2). Double click the left mouse button to load Publisher.

Figure 1.2 Publisher desktop icon

7 Publisher's Catalog appears (Figure 1.3). If it does not, then you will see a blank page as in Figure 1.5.

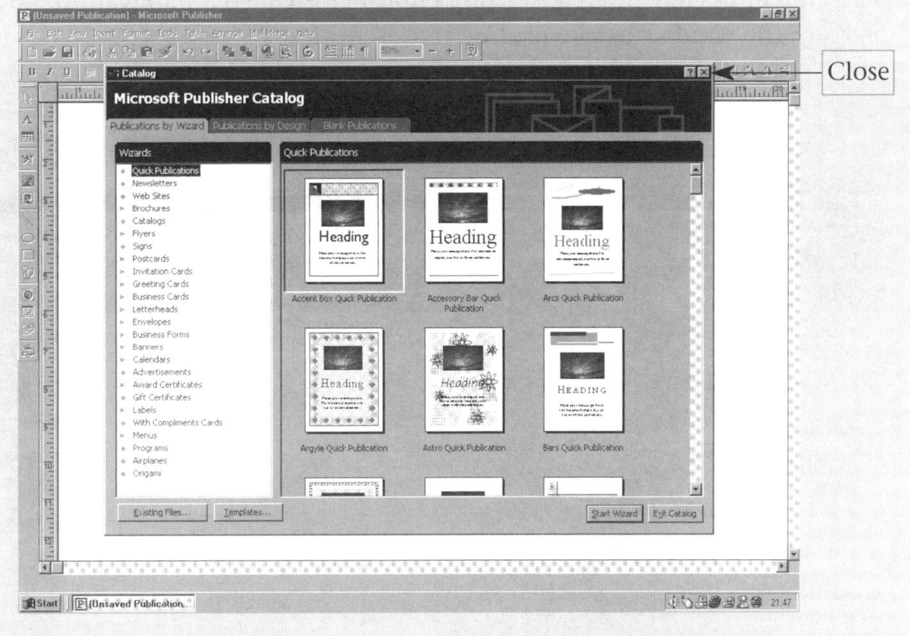

Figure 1.3 Publisher's opening window

Information

The **Catalog** is a series of ready-made page layouts (called wizards) that you can customise to your own requirements. For the purposes of this unit you will not be using the Catalog, as you are required to set up pages yourself.

1 To close the Catalog click on [X] as shown in Figure 1.3. Publisher's publication window appears (Figure 1.5).

2 Click on [Hide Wizard] in the bottom left corner of the window to hide the Quick Publication Wizard that may appear. (It may not appear.)

Information

To avoid having to close the Quick Publication Wizard every time you start a new file, you can turn it off. To do this:

1 Click on the **Tools** menu and select **Options**.

2 Click on the **User Assistance** tab (Figure 1.4).

Figure 1.4 Turn off Wizard

3 If there is a tick in the checkbox **Use Quick Publication Wizard for blank publications**, click in the box. The tick disappears.

4 Click **OK**.

If you are unable to do this on your system, you will need to close the Catalog every time.

Information: Identify parts of the publication window

Each file or document created using Publisher is called a publication. Locate each of the following parts of the window before reading its description.

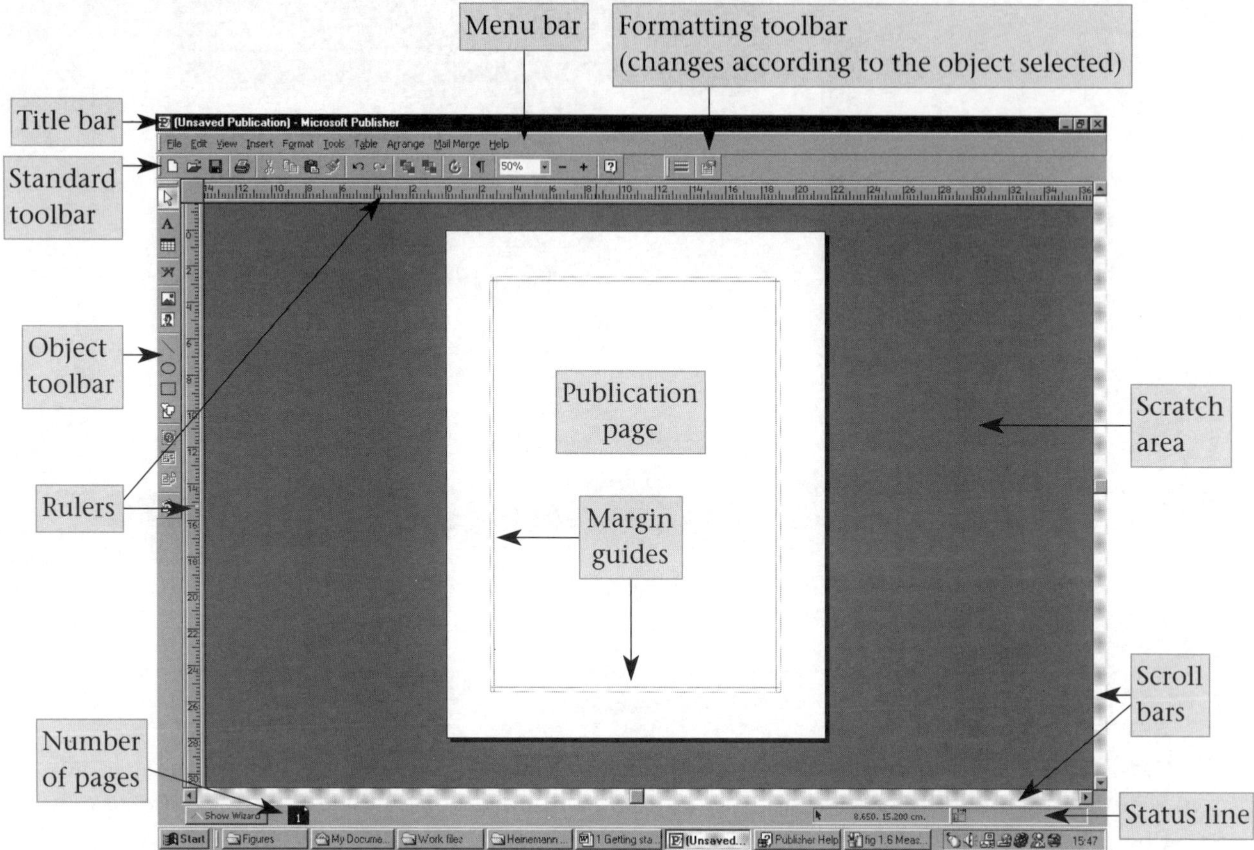

Figure 1.5 The publication window

- **Title bar** This displays the name of the current publication. (It is currently not named.)
- **Menu bar** Menus can be selected by clicking with the mouse or via the keyboard. Each menu drops down to give further options. This list will change according to the items you have most recently selected. You can click on [button] at the bottom of a menu to expand the list of options.
- **Toolbars** If you position the mouse over a button and wait, a **Screen Tip** will appear giving an explanation of its function.
  The **Standard toolbar** across the top of the window features shortcut buttons for frequently used actions such as **Save** and **Print**.
  The **Formatting toolbar** probably shares a row with the Standard toolbar, and is used for changing the appearance of objects. This toolbar will change depending on the object that is selected. For example, if text is selected, it will display options for changing the size and style of text. Sometimes these toolbars hold the more frequently used buttons but can be expanded to show more by clicking on **More Buttons** [button] at the end. (More Buttons does not currently display at this point.)
  The **Object toolbar** (by default, down the left side of the window) holds tools for creating different objects, such as text frames, or inserting clip art images.
- **Horizontal ruler** This aids accurate placement of objects on the page. There is also a **Vertical ruler** down the left side. If it is not visible, select **Rulers** from the **View** menu. →

- **Status bar** This displays the number of pages with the current page being highlighted (shown in black), the position of the pointer on the page and the size of an object.
- **Publication page** This is where you lay out text and images etc. to create your publication.
- **Margins** These are guides that mark out an area for you to work within, although you can place text and graphics outside them if you want to.
- **Scratch area** This is sometimes known as the desktop. Use this area to temporarily place objects whilst deciding where to position them on the page. Move them on and off the page until you are happy with the end result. Any objects on the scratch area when a file is saved are also saved.
- **Scroll bars** These are used for moving around the page and are particularly useful when zoomed in.

Information

Before starting work, you should check your settings to match those used in these instructions. See Tasks 1.2 and 1.3.

Task 1.2 Set measurement units

Method

1 Click on the **Tools** menu and select **Options**.

2 Click on the drop down arrow alongside **Measurement units** and click on centimeters (American spelling) if not already selected (Figure 1.6).

Options
General | Edit | User Assistance | Print
Start publication with page: 1
Measurement units: Centimeters

Figure 1.6 Measurement units

3 Click **OK**.

Task 1.3 Check paper and page size

You are likely to be using the most common paper size, A4, which is the size of this book. (You will learn more about paper sizes later.) A page can be set up as either portrait (tall) or landscape (wide).

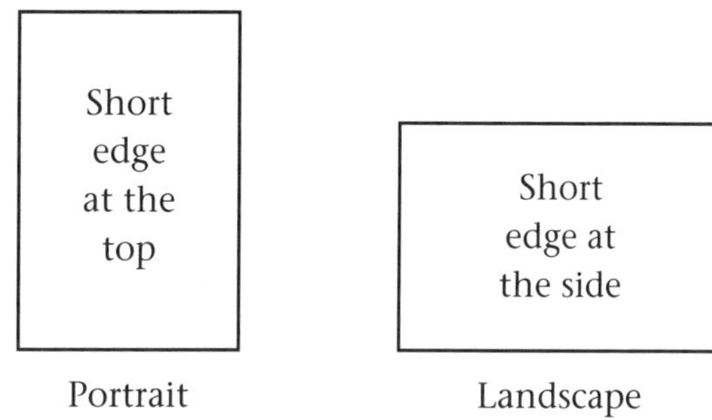

Print Setup determines the size of paper you will print on, and **Page Setup** determines the actual size of the document or publication if it should be different. For example, you may be printing on A4 but working on an A5 publication.

Method

1. Click on **File** menu and select **Print Setup**.
2. Click on drop down arrow alongside **Size** (Figure 1.7) and select **A4** if not already selected.
3. Click on the **Portrait** orientation button if not already selected. (A dot should be present on the button.)
4. Click **OK**.
5. Click on **File** menu and select **Page Setup**. (Page size is usually the same as the print size but it can be different.)
6. Check **Normal** layout is selected (Figure 1.8).
7. Check **Portrait** orientation is selected.
8. Click **OK**.

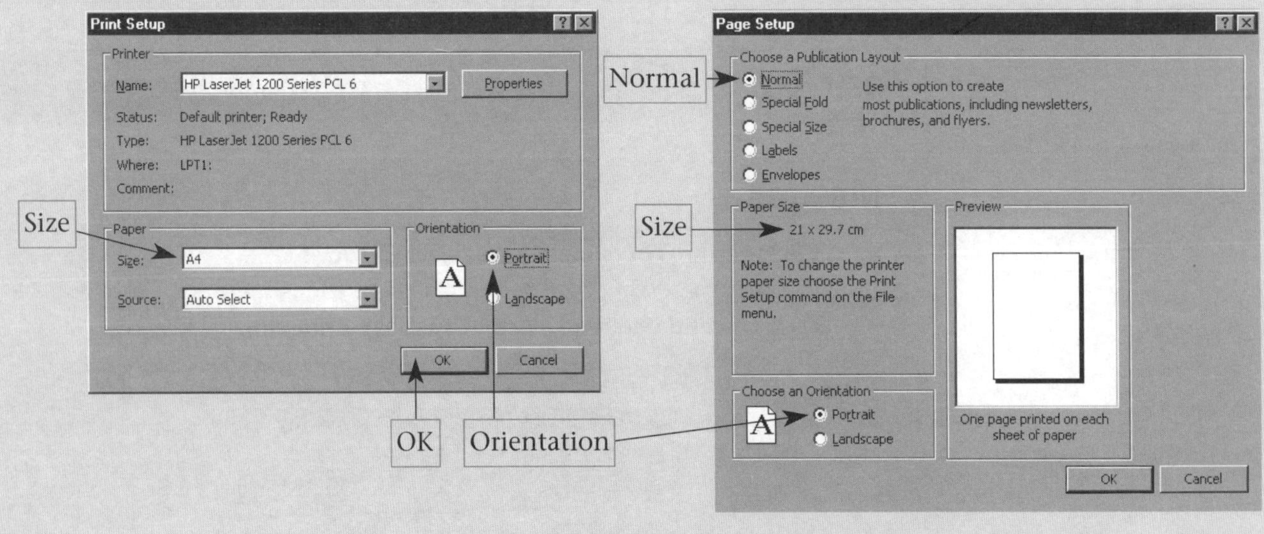

Figure 1.7 Print Setup

Figure 1.8 Page Setup

Task 1.4 Zoom in and out

When working with Publisher you will often need to move in closer to see what you are doing. Locate the **Zoom** buttons in the middle of the Standard toolbar (Figure 1.9).

Method

1. Click on the **Zoom in** button once and then again.
2. Click on **Zoom out**.
3. Click on the drop down arrow alongside the **Zoom** box and select **100%**.
4. Repeat, selecting **Page Width**.
5. Try other settings and end up at **50%** view.

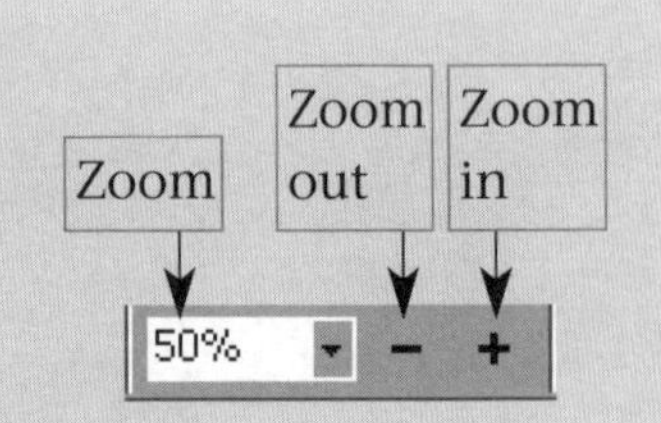

Figure 1.9 Zoom in and out

Task 1.5 Use the scroll bars

The **vertical scroll bar**, down the right-hand side of the window, and the **horizontal scroll bar**, across the bottom of the window, enable you to move around a publication, especially when you have zoomed in.

Method

1. To move up the page, click on the **Move up** arrow.
2. To move down the page, click on the **Move down** arrow.
3. Drag the grey box up or down.

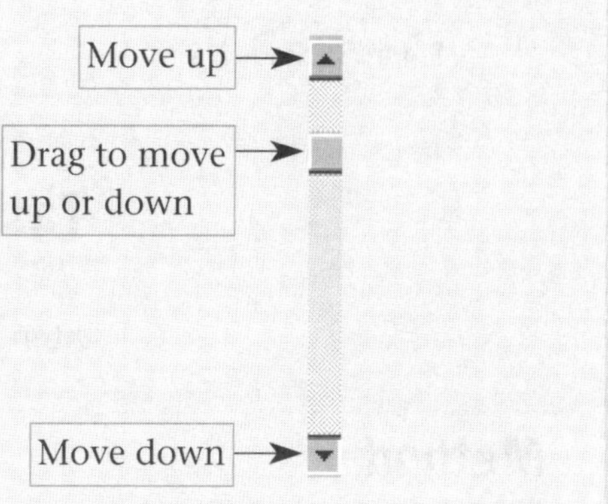

Figure 1.10 Vertical scroll bar

Task 1.6 Create a text frame

Method

1. Zoom to **Whole Page** view.
2. Click on the **Text Frame** tool **A** button (Figure 1.11) in the Object toolbar – pointer changes to a 'crosshair'.

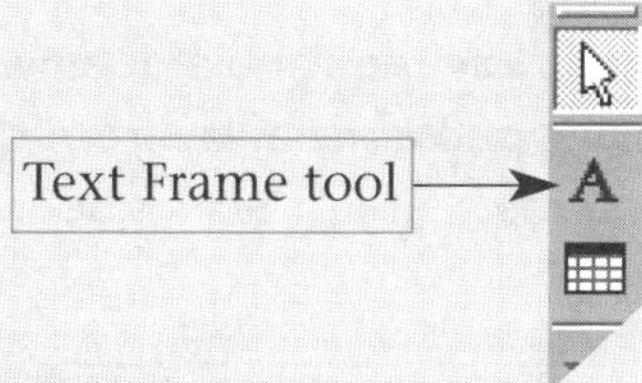

Figure 1.11 Text Frame tool

3. Position crosshair in the top left corner of the page on the blue margin guides.
4. Hold down the left mouse button and drag halfway across the page and down a little, then release. The text frame appears with selection handles in each corner and on the sides, and the cursor is flashing inside. **Hint:** The cursor is a small, flashing, vertical line which indicates where text will appear when keyed in.
5. Zoom in to **Page Width** view.
6. Key in your name.
7. Draw another text frame elsewhere on the page and key in your name again.

8 Draw a deeper text frame and key in your address pressing **Enter** (Figure 1.12) to start each new line.

Figure 1.12 Enter key

Task 1.7 Resize a text frame

Often you will need to change the size of a text frame.

Method

1 Click inside one of the text frames so the selection handles show.
2 Position the mouse pointer over the bottom middle handle – it changes to a resize handle.

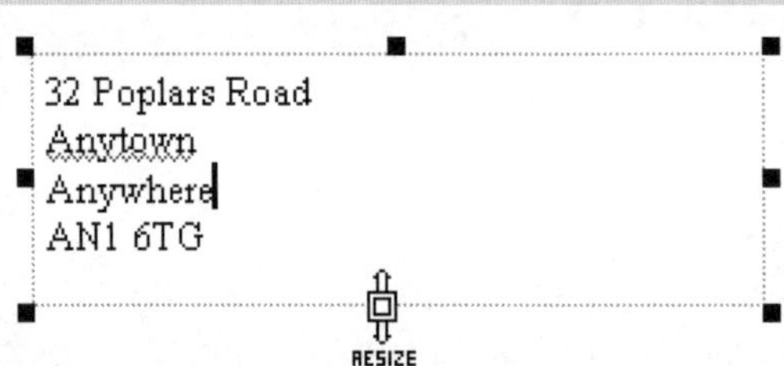

Figure 1.13 Resize a text frame

3 Hold the left mouse button down and drag the handle downwards a little.
4 Try this on each of the handles moving outwards away from the text a little each time.
5 Now make the text frame smaller so the text just fits inside it.

Information

When entering continuous text, Publisher will automatically word wrap within a text frame which means that as text reaches the right-hand side of the text frame, the next word will move onto the following line.

Task 1.8 Save a publication

When saving a publication always use a name that reflects the contents so you can identify it later. Filenames can comprise upper or lower case letters, numbers or other characters except / \ > < * ? " | : ;.

Method

1. Click on the Save button
2. The Save As dialogue box appears (Figure 1.14).

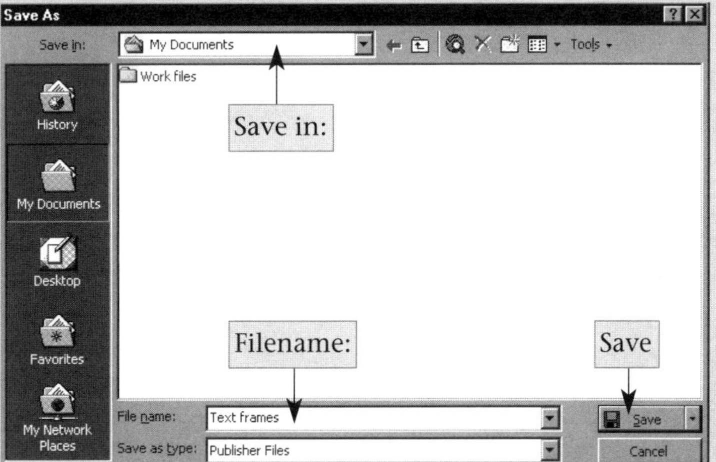

Figure 1.14 Save

The **Save in** box indicates where the file will be saved. By default this will be to My Documents or My Work, or to an area of a network assigned to you.

3. Click in the **File name:** box. Key in **Text frames** as the filename.
4. Click on **Save**.

Notice how the filename appears in the blue title bar at the top of the window.

Information

The onscreen version of a file is called the **soft copy** and a printout is called the **hard copy**.

Task 1.9 Print the publication

Method

Click on the **Print** button . One copy of your publication is sent to the printer.

Task 1.10 Close the publication

Method

Click on the **File** menu – select **Close**.

Task 1.11 Create a new publication, enter text, save, print, close

When keying in text, ignore any wavy lines that may appear under some words. You will learn about this in the next section.

Method

1 Click on the **New** publication button

2 Select the **Text Frame** tool and draw a text frame to fill the top half of the page.

3 Zoom to **Page Width** view.

4 Key in the following, pressing **Enter** twice after each line to leave a line space:

STAFF SOCIAL CLUB
Day Trip to France
July 27th
Leaving Staff Car Park at 7.00 am
Returning at 11.45 pm
£11.50 per person
See Dave Williams in Personnel for more details

5 Save the publication using the filename **Trip to France**.

6 Print.

7 Close the publication.

Task 1.12 Close Publisher

Method

Click on **File** menu – select **Exit**.

Task 1.13 Close down the computer

Method

1 On a home or standalone computer, click on **Start** menu (Figure 1.15).

2 Select **Shut Down**.

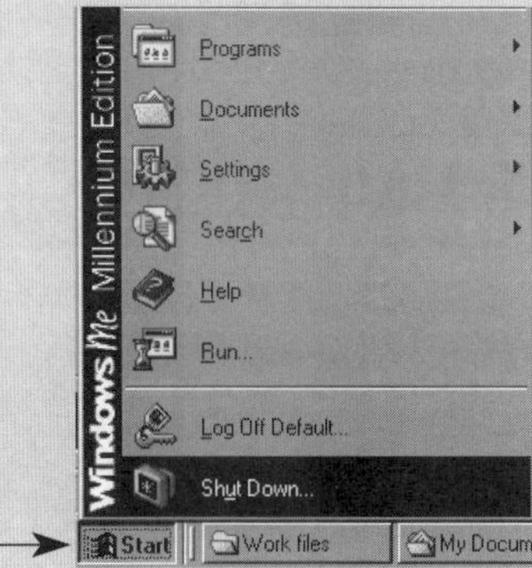

Figure 1.15 Start – Shut Down

3 Click on **OK** if dialogue box reads **Shut down** as in Figure 1.16.
If not, click on the down arrow and select **Shut down** from the list.

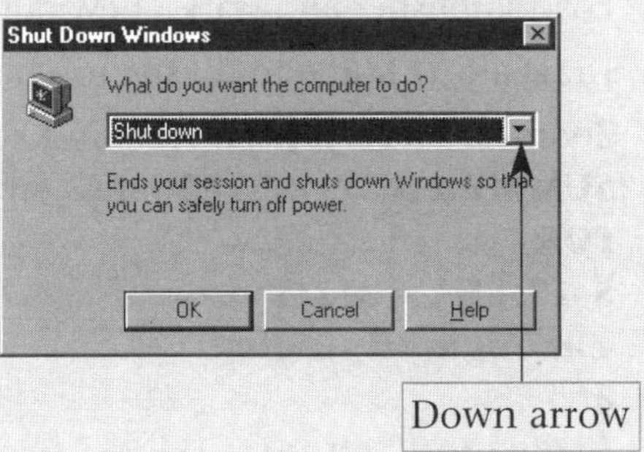

Figure 1.16 Shut down

4 Switch off.

On a network computer you must **log off** – check with your supervisor/tutor. Make a note of what you have to do.

Hint: When working on a network, never switch off at the mains socket unless told to, as you may switch off other users' computers.

→ Practise your skills 1

1. Load Publisher and start a new blank publication.
2. Draw a text frame to fill the top half of the page.
3. Zoom to **Page Width** view and key in the following text, pressing Enter twice after each line:
   Causeway Motors
   Full Servicing Facilities
   MOT Testing Station
   Repairs to all makes of cars
   Breakdown and Recovery Service
   The Causeway (press Enter once)
   Bishopsford
4. Resize the text frame if necessary.
5. Save the publication as **Causeway Motors**.
6. Print.
7. Close the publication.

→ Practise your skills 2

1 Load Publisher and start a new publication.
2 Draw a text frame to fill the top half of the page.
3 Zoom to **Page Width** view and key in the following text:
SUMMER ACTIVITIES (press Enter twice after each line)
FOR
5–12 YEAR OLDS
Throughout August
at
Kingsland School
A range of activities:
Swimming (press Enter once after the following lines)
Tennis
Football
Badminton
Team Games
Trampolining
Gymnastics (press Enter twice)
Pick up an application form from reception now
4 Resize the text frame if necessary.
5 Save the publication as **Summer Activities**.
6 Print.
7 Close the publication.

→ Check your knowledge

1 Is portrait paper wide or tall?
2 What is a soft copy?
3 What is the name given to a file or document in Publisher?
4 What is the scratch area?
5 How do you specify the size of paper you will be using?

Section 2 Editing text

You will learn to

- Open an existing publication
- Use the spellcheck
- Quick save a publication
- Move around a text frame
- Carry out basic editing – delete and insert text
- Use Undo and Redo
- Use Save As

Editing text involves changing the text content of a publication. In this section you will delete (remove) letters and words and insert new ones.

Task 2.1 Open existing publication

Method

1 Switch on your computer and load Publisher.
2 Click on **Open** button
3 Select **Trip to France**.
4 Click on **Open** (Figure 2.1).
5 The file opens.

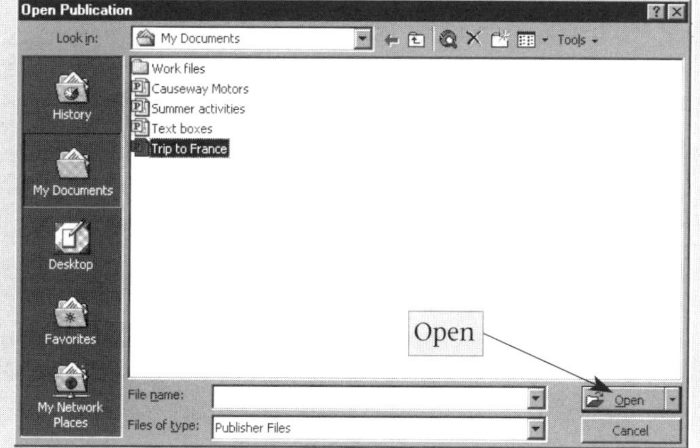

Figure 2.1 Open existing file

Information: Checking your work

When preparing any document it is important that the end result should be accurate and it is therefore essential to get into the habit of ensuring this right from the start. **Spellchecking** is one way of helping you to achieve this.

Spellchecking

Word has an automatic spellcheck that checks each word of your publication against an in-built dictionary. As you enter text, any word it does not recognise will appear on screen with a red wavy line underneath, e.g. your own name. This does not necessarily mean that it is wrong but the spellcheck does not recognise it. The word may not be in the dictionary or it may be a proper name. Do not totally rely on the spellcheck as it does not spot words that are correctly spelt but used in the wrong context, e.g. I am going four a walk, or I am going two go with ewe. It does not check whether your sentences make sense either or whether they convey the right meaning. Use the spellcheck but always read through your work carefully too, before and after printing. This is called proofreading.

Task 2.2 Spellcheck the document

Method

1. Click on the text frame. Selection handles appear on the sides and corners. **Note:** You must have a text frame selected before using the spellcheck.
2. Click on **Tools** menu and select **Spelling**.
3. From the side menu, select **Check Spelling**.
4. The Check Spelling dialogue box appears (Figure 2.2) unless you have no errors!
5. The spellchecker scans through the text frame stopping at any words it does not recognise and displays them in the Spellcheck dialogue box.

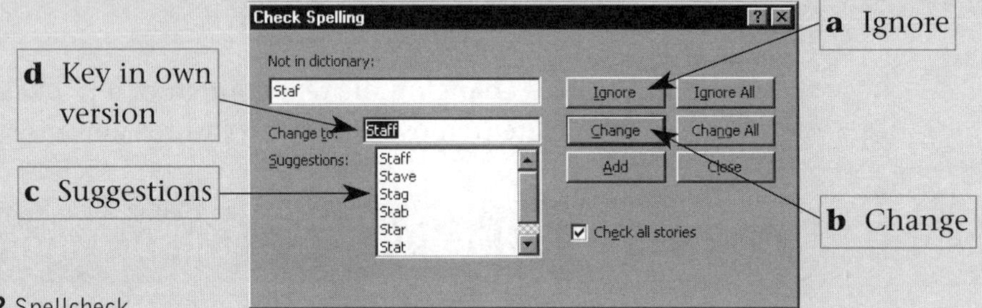

Figure 2.2 Spellcheck

6. Either:
   a Click on **Ignore** if you are satisfied with the spelling *or*
   b Click on **Change** to accept the highlighted suggested spelling *or*
   c Click on another **Suggestion** in the list and then click on **Change** *or*
   d Key in your own version of the word and click on **Change**.
7. The spellcheck continues through the text frame repeating the process. When it has finished, a message confirms the spellcheck is complete. Click **OK**. If you have more than one text frame, the following message may appear to which you should respond by clicking on Yes.

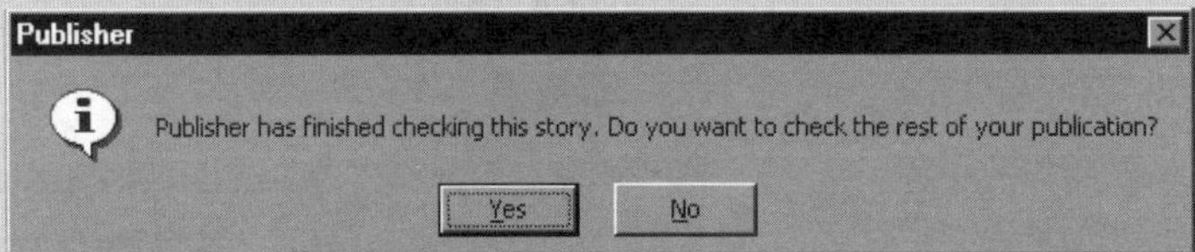

Figure 2.3 Check rest of publication

If you had no errors in your publication, return to this section when you next need to use the spellcheck.

Hint:

It is also possible to **Add** words to the dictionary that you use frequently, such as proper names.

From now on you should always use the spellcheck and proofread your work.

Task 2.3 Quick save the file

Once a publication file has been saved and named, click on the Save button to resave it at any time. Any amendments are saved, overwriting the original file. It is good practice to save your work every ten minutes using this method in case a system error or power failure occurs. You would then only lose work produced since you last saved.

Method

Click on **Save** button 

Information: Moving around a text frame

There are several ways of moving around a text frame. Click into the text and try these now.

- **Use the mouse** As you move the mouse over the text it takes on the appearance of an I-beam. Move it to the required position and click the left mouse button once. The cursor will appear at that point.
- **Use the keyboard** Towards the right of the main keyboard is a bank of four arrow keys (Figure 2.4). Pressing one of the keys causes the cursor to move up, down, left or right accordingly. Holding a key down speeds up the movement. Press **End** to move to the end of a line and **Home** to move to the start.

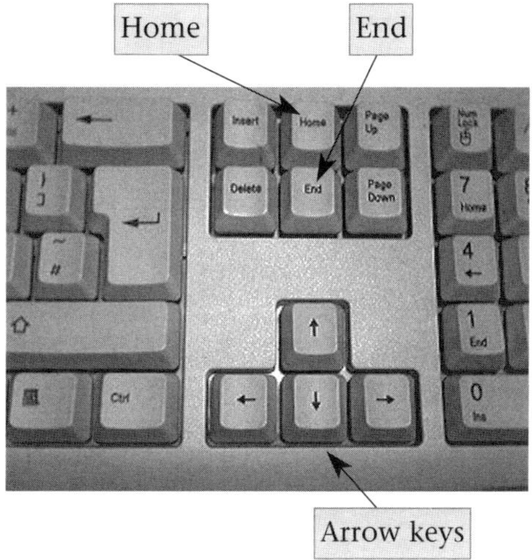

Figure 2.4 Moving around

Information: Editing

Editing means to change the content of a publication. This might involve altering words or characters by deleting, inserting, copying or moving them around. Graphics and images can also be edited.

Task 2.4 Delete text

Characters can be deleted to the left of the cursor position or to the right.

To delete to the left of the cursor Press the Backspace key (Figure 2.5).
To delete to the right of the cursor Press the Delete key.

Figure 2.5 Backspace and Delete keys

Method

1. Position the cursor directly after the word **Staff** in the fourth line. Press the **Backspace** key once. Repeat until the word **Staff** and the space in front of it have been deleted.
2. Position the cursor directly in front of the word **in** in the last line. Press the **Delete** key once. Repeat until the words **in Personnel** and the space following have been deleted.
3. Save the file.

Information

To delete a text frame, click on it to select and choose **Delete object** from the **Edit** menu.

Task 2.5 Insert text

Text can be inserted by positioning the cursor where the text is required and keying it in. The text to the right of the cursor moves across making space for the new word/s.

Method

1. Position the cursor directly in front of **11.45 pm** in the fifth line. Key in the word **approximately** and press the spacebar to leave a space.
2. Position the cursor directly in front of the word **Car** in the fourth sentence. Key in the words **the Visitors** and leave a space.
3. Position the cursor directly in front of the word **for** in the last line and key in **in Marketing**. Press the spacebar.
4. Position the cursor after **£11.50 per person**, press **Enter** and key in **In Euros €18.40!**
5. Spellcheck your document and proofread the document onscreen making any necessary corrections.
6. Save your file.

Hint:

To key in the Euro sign €, hold down the **Alt Gr** key to the right of the spacebar and press **4** (Alt Gr + 4). If you do not have an Alt Gr key, then hold down **Ctrl** and **Alt** to the left of the spacebar together, and press **4** (Ctrl + Alt + 4).

Task 2.6 Use Undo and Redo

Everybody makes mistakes sometimes and you may, for example, delete some text and then change your mind. Publisher has a very useful feature that remembers the last few changes you made and allows you to reverse them. It will let you undo a change and also allow you to redo it! Each time you click on Undo it will take you back one more stage (Figure 2.6).

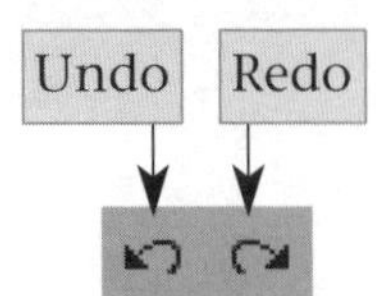

Figure 2.6 Undo and Redo

Method

1 Highlight the word **Williams** in the last line and press **Delete**.
2 Click on **Undo** – the action is undone and the word reappears.
3 Click on **Redo** – the word disappears.
4 Click on **Undo** – the word reappears.

Ensure you end up with the word **Williams** showing.

Information: Save As

So far you have used the Save button to save publications. The first time a publication is saved, you must name it. When you subsequently save it by the same method, you are not prompted for a name as it already has one. Any changes you have made overwrite the original.

There may, however, be occasions when you wish to save a new version of a publication with any amendments, but keep the original document intact. This is when you use **Save As**, meaning you **Save** a publication or file **As** something else, i.e. by another name. The new name can be similar or completely different, but of course should always reflect the content. **Save As** can also be used for saving a publication to another location.

Task 2.7 Save a publication using a new name

You are going to save **Trip to France** with a new name to preserve the original publication. Note the existing name in the title bar at the top of the screen before you do this.

Method

1 Using the open file **Trip to France**, select **Save As** from the **File** menu. The Save As window opens.

Save As
Save in: My Documents
Tools
History
My Documents
Desktop
Favorites
My Network Places
Causeway Motors
Summer activities
Text boxes
Trip to France
File name: Trip to France 2
Save as type: Publisher Files
Save
Cancel

Figure 2.7 Save As

2 Key in the filename **Trip to France 2**.
3 Click on **Save**. Note the new name in the title bar.
4 Print and close the file.

→ Practise your skills 1

1. Open the publication **Causeway Motors**.
2. Delete the word **Service** in the fifth line.
3. Delete the **s** from **Motors** in the first line.
4. Insert the word **Company** after **Motor** in the first line. (You may need to leave a space first.)
5. Insert the word **Speedy** in front of **Repairs** in the fourth line.
6. Delete the capital **R** of **Repairs** in the same line and replace with a lower case **r**.
7. Insert **24 Hour** in front of **Breakdown** in the fifth line and leave a space. Save the publication as **Causeway Motors 2**.
8. Spellcheck and proofread, saving again if more changes are made.
9. Print.
10. Close the publication.

→ Practise your skills 2

1. Open the publication **Summer activities**.
2. Insert the word **Junior** in front of **School** in the fifth line.
3. Delete the word **Trampolining** in the list of activities and replace with **Athletics**.
4. Insert the words **fully supervised** in front of activities in the seventh line.
5. Delete the words **an application form** in the last line and replace with **a leaflet**.
6. Save the publication using the name **Summer activities 2**.
7. Spellcheck and proofread, saving again if more changes are made.
8. Print.
9. Close the publication.

→ Check your knowledge

1. How often should you save a publication and why?
2. You should always spellcheck your work but why should you not rely on the spellcheck alone?
3. What is this button used for? 
4. What is this button used for? 
5. What is the difference between Save and Save As?

Section 3 Formatting text

You will learn to

- Select text
- Format and emphasise text
  - ☐ Change font
  - ☐ Change font size
  - ☐ Understand text overflow
- Move a toolbar
- Change text alignment
- Change font colour
- Move a text frame

Formatting text means changing the appearance of text, not the content. In this section you will find out how to select text and then to format it. You will also handle text frames as objects.

Information

Presentation is very important in desktop publishing and there are many ways of presenting text. This is often carried out by changing selected areas of text and it is therefore useful to look at ways of selecting text before going any further.

To select:	**Method**
One word	Double click on word (also selects the following space)
Several words	Press and drag the I-beam across several words and release (Figure 3.1)
To deselect	Click anywhere off the text

Task 3.1 Select text

Method

1. Open the publication **Text frames**.
2. Position the cursor directly in front of the text to be selected – here, it is the postcode **AN1 6TG**, but you can use your own address.
3. Hold down the left mouse button and drag the I-beam across both words and the following space. The text appears to be highlighted (Figure 3.1).

Hint:

Selecting text is often known as highlighting.

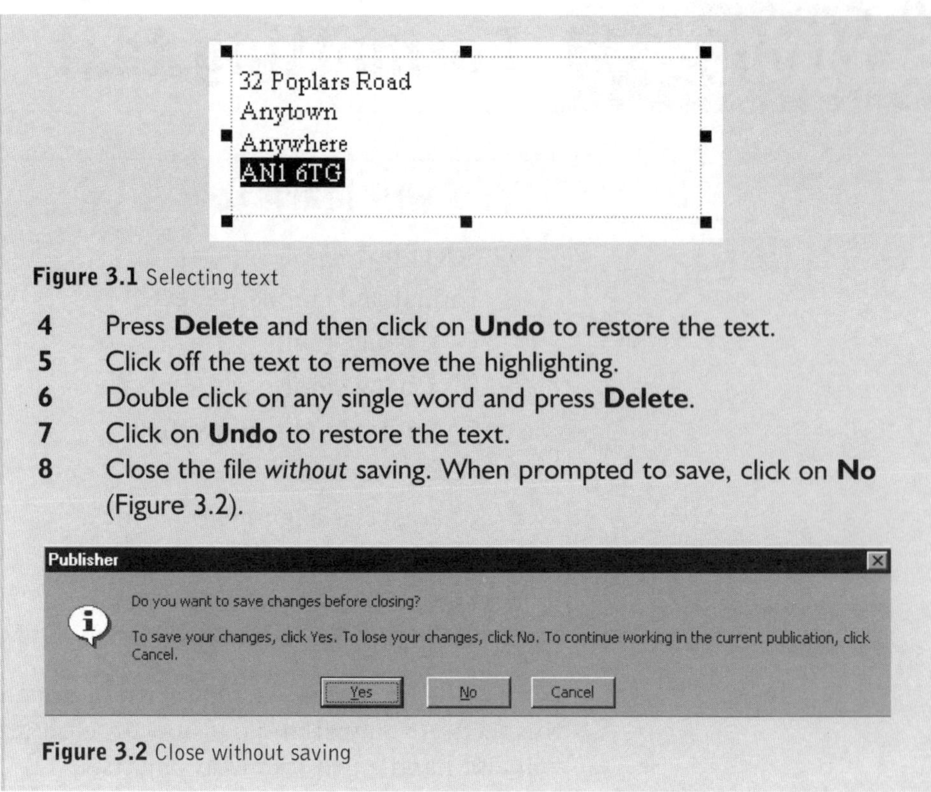

Figure 3.1 Selecting text

4 Press **Delete** and then click on **Undo** to restore the text.
5 Click off the text to remove the highlighting.
6 Double click on any single word and press **Delete**.
7 Click on **Undo** to restore the text.
8 Close the file *without* saving. When prompted to save, click on **No** (Figure 3.2).

Figure 3.2 Close without saving

Information: Formatting text

A desktop publishing package makes it easy to produce well-presented publications and text is an important part of that. Formatting text might involve changing the size of text, the font style or enhancing particular key points to give them emphasis and make them stand out from the rest of the text. Here are some examples:

Font	Most fonts are either **serif** or **sans serif**. Serifs are little strokes at the ends of characters which sans serif characters do not have. The default font in Word is **Times New Roman** which is a serif font. **Arial** is an example of sans serif. Both fonts are suitable for standard business documents, although serif fonts are considered easier when reading lengthy documents. There are a huge number of fonts available, e.g. , Mistral, Verdana and Jokerman. They can be traditional, formal, serious, informal, fun, quirky, friendly etc. Choose carefully according to the message you have to convey.
Font size	Size 10 or 12 is the usual default size for body text but can be varied, especially for headings and subheadings and also for special purposes, e.g. advertisements. Font sizes are measured in points – the higher the number, the larger the font, e.g. 16 point, 18 point, 20 point. Different fonts can appear to be different sizes even set at the same size.
CAPITALS	Capitals are used to make words stand out, especially headings.
Bold	The term 'to embolden text' means to make it bold, which is heavier and darker than normal text. Bold is frequently used to make words more noticeable – especially headings.
Italics	Italics are also used for emphasis, usually within the main body of a document.
Underline	Underline is not used as much as bold, but is useful for giving emphasis to particular words in the main body of a document, and sometimes for headings.

Information

The **Formatting** toolbar (Figure 3.3) holds the necessary buttons for fonts, size and emphasis. It is only visible when you are working with text.

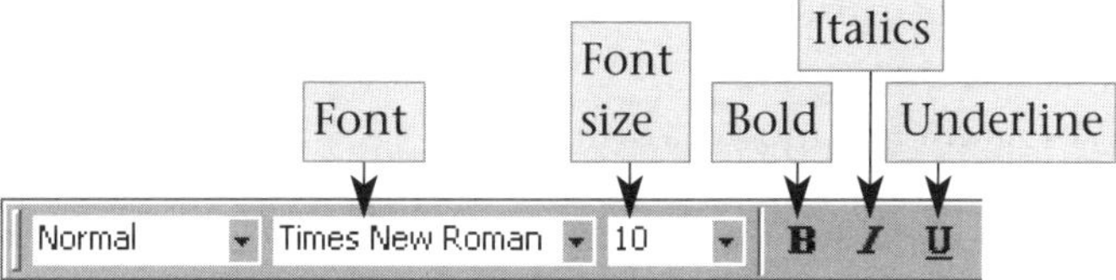

Figure 3.3 Formatting toolbar

To format text by changing font or font size Select existing text and click on the arrow alongside either Font or Font size to reveal a drop down list of fonts and sizes (Figure 3.4). You can also key in a size in between those offered, e.g. 11. For a choice of fonts scroll through the font list by clicking on the up and down scroll buttons (Figure 3.5).

Figure 3.4 Fonts

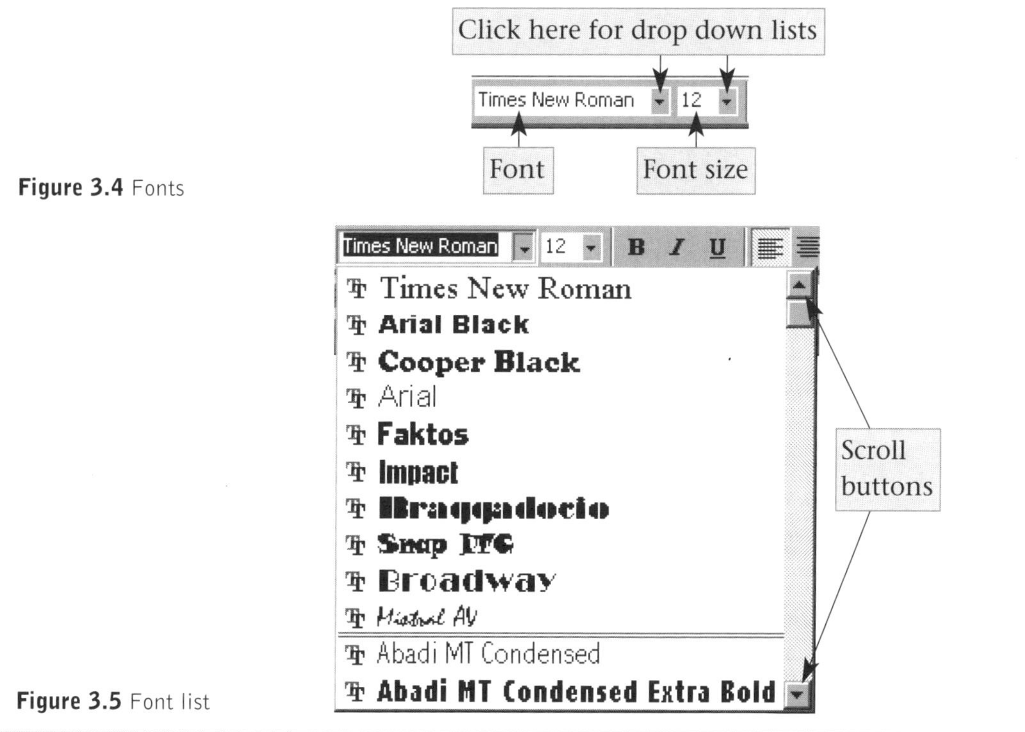

Figure 3.5 Font list

Task 3.2 Format text

Method

1. Open the file **Trip to France 2**.
2. Select the words **Staff Social Club**.
3. Click on the **font** drop down list, scroll through and select the font **Arial**.
4. With the text still selected, click on the **font size** drop down list and select **36**.
5. Select the remaining text and change it to **Tempus Sans ITC** or **Comic Sans MS**.
6. Select the second and third lines and change the size to **36**.
7. Select the next two lines and change the size to **36**.
8. Select the remaining lines of text and change the size to **24**.
9. Save the publication using the existing name.

Note: See next page if the lines are no longer visible

Information: Text overflow

Depending on the size of your text frame, you may find that the last lines of text can now no longer be seen. This is because the text you have formatted is now bigger and it is taking up more space. As there is no room left in the text frame, it is being held in an area called **overflow** (Figure 3.6). You must make the text frame bigger by dragging on the bottom middle selection handle to show the remaining lines. (You can also drag side handles outwards.)

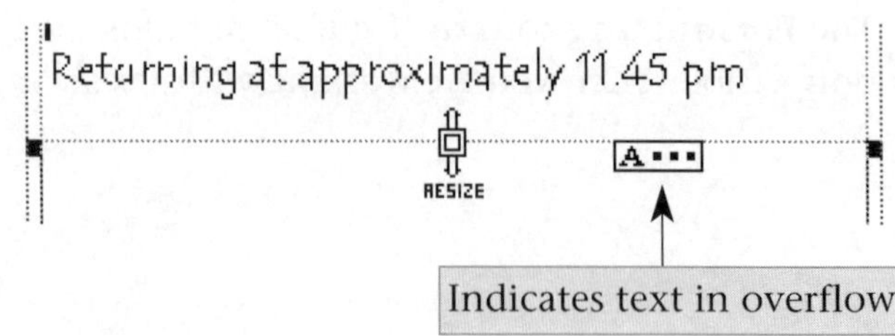

Figure 3.6 Text overflow

Information: Emphasise text

To format text by changing style of emphasis Highlight existing text and click on the **Bold**, **Italics** or **Underline** button as required (Figure 3.7).

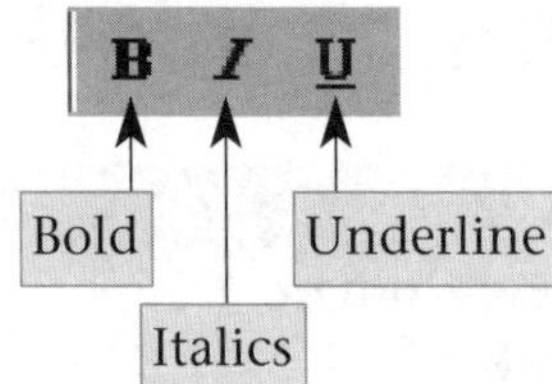

Figure 3.7 Emphasis

You can also select one of these options by clicking on it before keying in new text, and then deselect it by clicking on it again afterwards.

Task 3.3 Apply emphasis to text

Method

1. Select the first three lines of text including the date and click on **Bold** **B**
2. Select the text **£11.50 per person** and click on the **Bold** button and then the **Italics** *I* button.
3. Select the text **7.30 am** and click on the underline button U
4. Repeat for the text **11.45 pm**.
5. Save the file.

Task 3.4 Move a toolbar

You are going to work with more of the options on the Formatting toolbar which currently shares a row with the Standard toolbar. You will now move it so that you can see the full toolbar. Ensure you have clicked into a text frame first.

Move handle

Figure 3.8 Move toolbar

Method

1. Click on the **Move** handle at the left end of the **Formatting** toolbar (Figure 3.8). The pointer changes to a four-headed arrow
2. Holding the left mouse button down, drag just *slightly* downwards and to the left and the toolbar should move to the line below if it becomes detached.

Information: Format text – text alignment

Text is, by default, aligned to the left. This means that the left margin is straight but the right-hand side is 'ragged' – each line ending at a different point. This paragraph is an example of text that is **left aligned** or **left justified**. It is also sometimes known as ragged right or unjustified.

This paragraph has **fully justified** margins, which means that the margins are straight on both sides. Publisher adjusts the words and spaces so that each line stretches across the page to end at the right margin. The exception is the last line of the paragraph, which would look odd if spaced across the page.

Normal continuous text is aligned left or justified.

Centred text is centred between the left and right edge of the text frame. It is not used for continuous text but may be used for headings or displaying text, e.g.

HERE IS A CENTRED HEADING

Aligned right or **right justified** causes each line to end at the right margin. It is not used as often as other alignments but can be used for display purposes.

The **Formatting toolbar** also holds the necessary buttons for **alignment** (Figure 3.9).

To change alignment Highlight existing text to be aligned and click on the appropriate button.

Alignment options can also be selected before keying in new text.

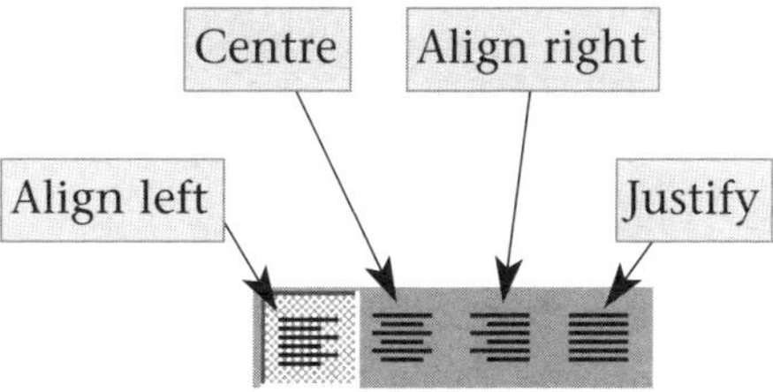

Figure 3.9 Alignment

Task 3.5 Align text

Method

1. Using the same publication (Trip to France 2), select all lines of text and click on the Centre button
2. Save the publication.

Task 3.6 Change font colour

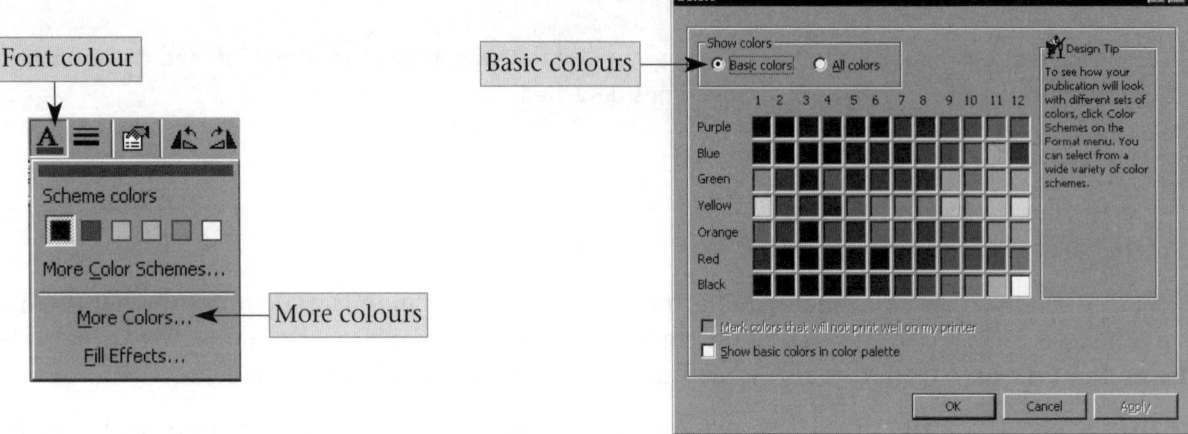

Figure 3.10 Change font colour

Figure 3.11 Colour palette

Hint:

When you have selected a colour it is made available when you first click on the Font Color button.

Hint:

Use colour carefully – too many colours distract from the message. Pale colours make text difficult to read.

Method

1. Using the same publication select all the text.
2. Click on the **Font Color** button on the Formatting toolbar.
3. Click on **More Colors** (Figure 3.10).
4. Click on Basic Colors if not already selected (Figure 3.11).
5. Click on a blue colour and click **OK**.
6. Select the date and change it to a red colour.
7. Repeat for the times and the price.
8. Save the publication.

Task 3.7 Move a text frame

Hint:

Make sure you keep away from selection handles when moving an object.

Note:

The process of moving any object is the same as this.

Method

1. Ensure the text frame is selected (i.e. handles appear). Position the pointer over the edge of the frame. The **Move object** symbol appears (Figure 3.12).

Figure 3.12 Move object

2. Hold the left mouse button down and drag the text frame downwards so it is roughly in the centre of the page.
3. Save the publication.
4. Print and close.

Information

If you are working with other people it would be useful to add your name to your work so you can identify your printouts. On all your work from now on, create a small text frame just below the margin in the bottom left of the page and key in your name.

→ Practise your skills 1

1 Open the publication **Causeway Motors 2**.
2 Change the font to **Arial**.
3 Increase the size of all text to **28**, resizing the text frame as necessary.
4 Centre all the text except the last two lines (the address).
5 Right align (right justify) the address.
6 Make the first line bold.
7 Underline the line that starts **24 hour** . . .
8 Put the address into italics.
9 Change the font colours of the text – you choose.
10 Move the text frame downwards so it is roughly in the centre.
11 Save the publication as **Causeway Motors 3**.
12 Print and close.

→ Practise your skills 2

1 Open the publication **Summer Activities 2**.
2 Change the font to a sans serif font of your choice.
3 Change the size of the first three lines to **28**.
4 Change the size of the remaining text to **18**.
5 Make the first three lines bold.
6 Underline the words **Throughout August**.
7 Align the list of activities to the right.
8 Change the font colour to one of your choice.
9 Save the publication as **Summer Activities 3**.
10 Print and close.

→ Check your knowledge

1 How do you select a single word?
2 What is the difference between a serif and a sans serif font?
3 What does this symbol mean? A ▪▪▪
4 What is the overflow area?
5 Explain each of the following: left justified, right justified, centred, fully justified.

Consolidation 1

1 Open a new blank publication.
2 Change the print setup to A5 landscape.
3 Draw a text frame to fill the page keeping within the margins.
4 Key in the following text:
Mobile Hairdresser (press Enter twice)
Fully trained and experienced hairdresser will visit you in your own home (press Enter twice)
Cuts
Blow drys
Tints
Perms (press Enter twice)
Lady and gentleman customers welcome (press Enter twice)
Competitive rates
20% reduction for your first appointment (press Enter twice)
Telephone Franki now on 0927324128
5 Proofread and spellcheck.
6 Save the publication as **Mobile Hair**.
7 Delete the words **Fully trained and**, and change the **e** of **experienced** to a capital letter.
8 Change the first line to size **18** and **bold**.
9 Change the second line to size **16**.
10 Change the remaining text to size **14**.
11 Centre the list of four services (**Cuts, Blow drys**, etc.) and make them bold.
12 Underline the words **20% reduction**.
13 Align the last line to the right and make it bold.
14 Change the font of the first line to a sans serif font.
15 Change the font of the remaining text to any of your choice, making sure all text is visible.
16 Change font colours as you feel fit.
17 Save the publication as **Mobile Hair 2**.
18 Print using A5 paper if you have it. If not, use A4.

Section 4 Working with images

You will learn to

- Insert clip art
- Resize and move clip art
- Search for clip art
- Delete clip art
- Insert graphics as files from CD or floppy disk
- Choose text wrap options

All parts of a publication are separate objects. The text frames you have worked with are objects and in this section you will be inserting graphical objects into your publications using clip art images which are supplied with Publisher. You should also ideally have an image file on floppy disk or CD.

Task 4.1 Insert clip art, resize and move

Method

1 Open a new publication.
2 Click on the **Clip Gallery** tool button in the left-hand side **Object** toolbar.
3 Move the mouse onto the page – the pointer changes to a crosshair.
4 Position the crosshair at the top of the page in the middle. Hold the left mouse button down and drag the crosshair to draw a frame.
5 **Insert Clip Art** window appears (Figure 4.1).

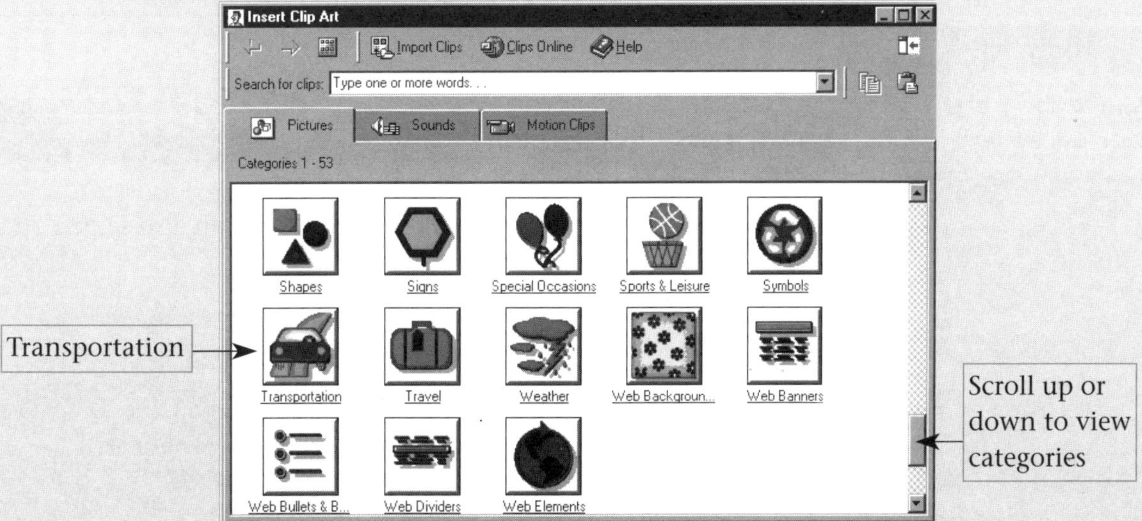

Figure 4.1 Clip art categories

6 Scroll down and click on the category, e.g. **Transportation**.
7 View the images by scrolling down and click on any one to select it (Figure 4.2). Your images may be different to those shown.

Figure 4.2 Insert clip art

8 Click on **Insert clip**.
9 Close Clip Art window by clicking on ☒. The image appears on the page with selection handles around the sides (Figure 4.3).
10 Position pointer over a corner handle (pointer changes to a resize handle) and drag inwards towards the middle of the image to make it smaller.
11 Position pointer over the image – it changes to a **Move** symbol. Hold down the left mouse button and drag the image to a new position on the left.
12 Repeat from step 2 above to place a second image on the right.
13 Do this twice more to insert more images and try resizing them and moving them around.
14 Save the publication as **Graphics**.

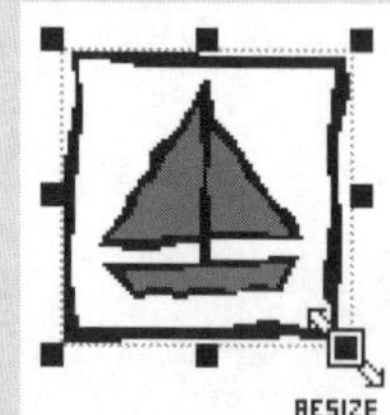

Figure 4.3 Resize image

Hint:

Always resize using a corner handle to keep the image in proportion.

Hint:

The Move symbol is the same for moving a text frame. 

Information

You can also nudge an image or text frame into position by selecting it, holding down the **Alt** key (to the left of the spacebar) and using the arrow keys on the keyboard.

Task 4.2 Search for clip art

As well as looking through clip art categories, you can also search on a keyword, e.g. car.

Method

1 Click on the **Clip Gallery** tool and draw a frame.
2 Key in **car** in the **Search for clips** box and press **Enter**.

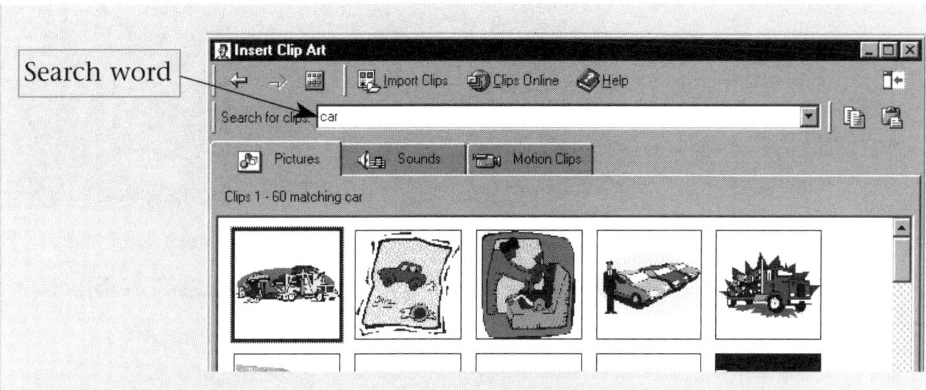

Figure 4.4 Search for clip art

3 From the images displayed (yours may be different), select one and click on **Insert clip** as before.
4 Close the Clip Art window.
5 Resize and reposition the image on the left.
6 Repeat from step 1 above to search for an image of a **hat**.
7 Resize and reposition the image on the right.
8 Try this again searching on a keyword of your own choice.
9 Save the publication.

Task 4.3 Delete clip art

Hint:

You can delete any graphic object in this way.

Method

1 Click on an image to select it.
2 Press **Delete** on the keyboard.

Information: Insert picture objects

Clip art may sometimes be supplied to you as a file on floppy disk or CD. You may also be asked to insert a photograph from a floppy disk or a CD.

Task 4.4 Insert graphics from CD or floppy disk

You will need an image file on floppy disk or CD for this task.

Method

1 Use the same publication (Graphics). If using a CD or floppy disk, insert into the appropriate drive (Figures 4.5 or 4.6).
- **For a CD**, press the button below the drive to open it and place CD onto the tray. Press the drive button for the tray to retract.
- **For a floppy disk**, push the disk gently into the drive.

Figure 4.5 CD drive

Figure 4.6 Floppy disk drive

2 Click on the **Picture Frame** tool in the left-hand side **Object** toolbar and draw a frame.

3 Double click inside the frame. **Insert Picture** window appears.

4 Click on the down arrow alongside **Look in**: box (Figure 4.7).

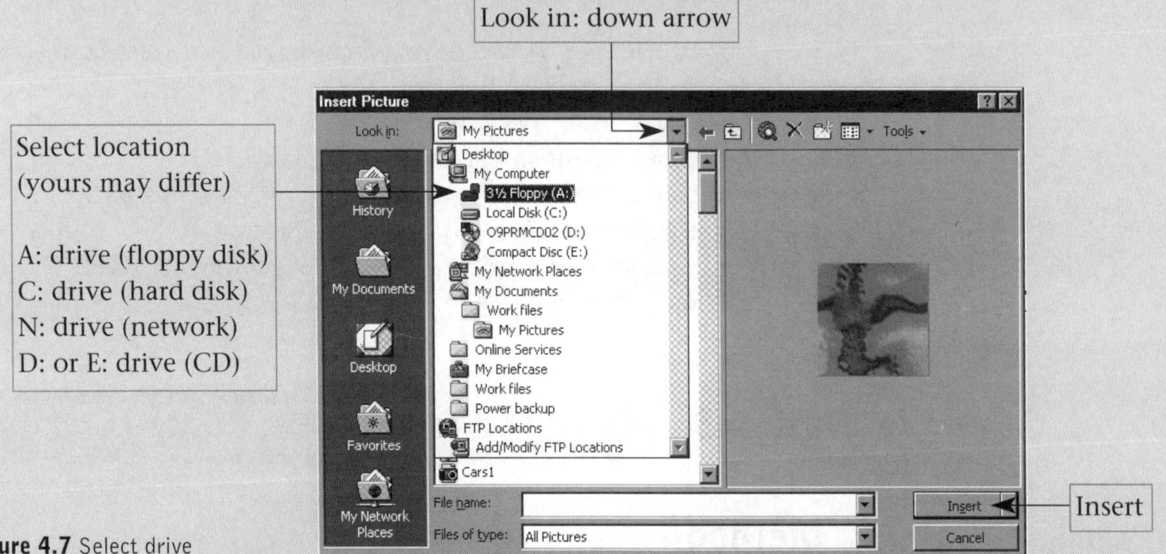

Figure 4.7 Select drive

5 Double click to select the required location. In this example **floppy disk drive A:** has been selected.

Figure 4.8 Select graphic image

6 Select image required and click on **Insert** (Figure 4.8).

7 The graphic image appears on the page. This image can be resized and moved in exactly the same way as clip art, either by selecting and dragging.

8 Save the publication, print and close.

To remove the floppy disk, push the small button which is usually directly below the drive and the disk is released. (Make sure you do not press the power button which may be nearby!)

To remove the CD, press the button below the drive to open it and remove. Press the button to retract the tray.

Information: Text wrap

When you place a graphic image onto a page you must consider whether you want the text to wrap around it or not. For the type of publication you have created so far, i.e. posters and adverts, you are likely to place images around the text, without wanting the position of the text to be affected, as in Figure 4.9. Look closely at Figure 4.10 and you will see that text wrap around objects has been applied – the text has moved away from the image. For continuous paragraphs of text, as in Figure 4.11, images are likely to be placed into the text and the text must wrap around them otherwise some text may be hidden.

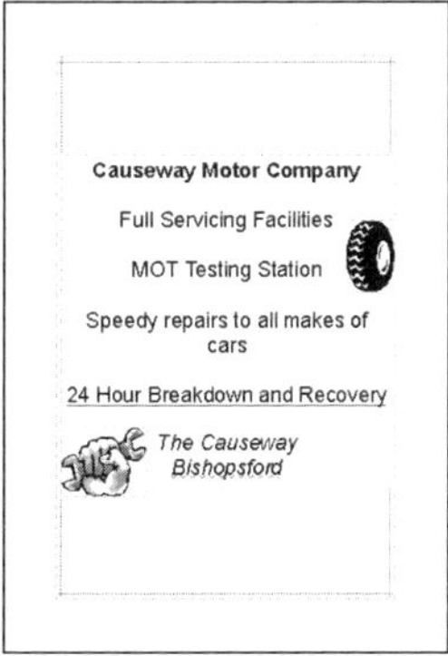

Figure 4.9
Without text wrap around objects

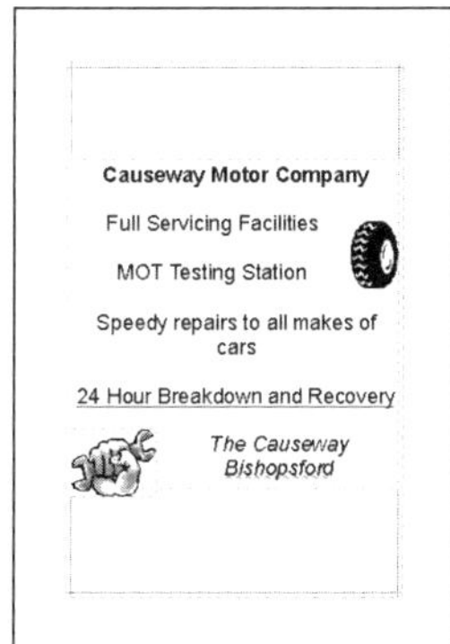

Figure 4.10
With text wrap around objects

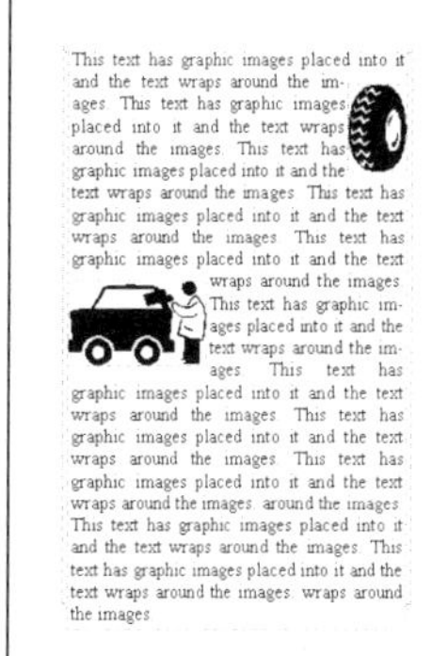

Figure 4.11
With text wrap around objects

Task 4.5 Choose text wrap options

Method

1. Open the publication **Trip to France 2**.
2. Search for a clip art image on the keyword **France**.
3. Place the image on the scratch area (off the page).
4. Search for another image on the keyword **ship** and place on the scratch area.
5. Click on the text to select the text frame and click on the **Text Frame Properties** button 
6. Click in check box beside **Wrap text around objects** (Figure 4.12).

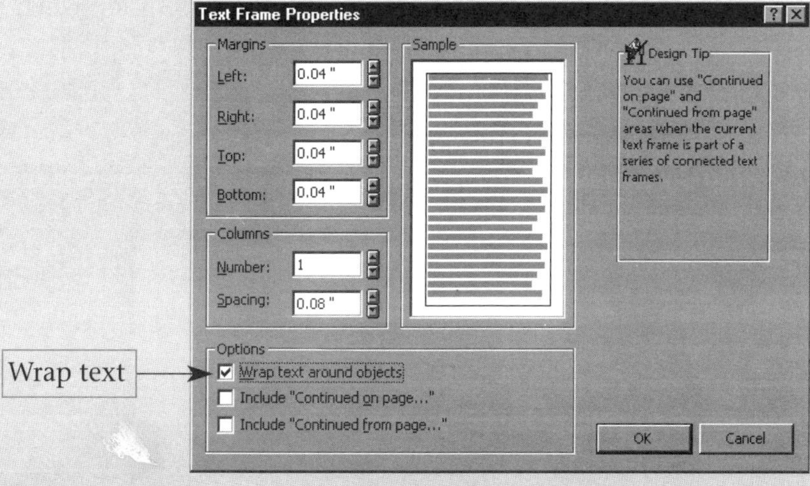

Figure 4.12 Text frame properties

7 Move one of the images alongside the text **July 27th** to see how the text behaves. (It should move!)
8 Click in the text frame and click on the **Text Frame Properties** button . Check off **Wrap text** around objects. (The text should move back into position and not be affected by the image.)
9 Move the second image to a position just below the last line of text.
10 Save as **Trip to France 3**, print and close the publication.

Hint:

You can also select Text Frame Properties from the Format menu.

→ Practise your skills 1

1 Open the publication **Causeway Motors 3**.
2 Ensure text wrap is off.
3 Search for three pieces of clip art using the search words **car**, **mechanic** and **wrench**.
4 Resize them to a suitable size.
5 Position one at the top of the page in the middle, one at the bottom on the right, and one opposite the address.
6 Save as **Causeway Motors 4**.
7 Print and close.

→ Practise your skills 2

1 Open the publication **Summer activities 3**.
2 Ensure text wrap is off.
3 Search for three pieces of clip art using suitable search words.
4 Resize them to a suitable size.
5 Position them in suitable positions on the page.
6 Save as **Summer activities 4**.
7 Print and close.

→ Check your knowledge

1 How can you resize clip art or other picture object?
2 How can you ensure it is kept in proportion when resizing it?
3 How do you nudge it into position?
4 What is the purpose of text wrap?
5 How do you apply it?

Has a Tutor seen your blue RECORD OF PROGRESS card recently?

IF NOT ASK A TUTOR TO CHECK YOUR PROGRESS NOW

Section 5 Working with folders

You will learn to

- Create and open folders
- Move files between folders
- Delete a publication/file
- Save into a folder
- Save to floppy disk

It is important that you learn how to organise your files on the computer just as you (hopefully) keep your paper files organised! In his section you will find out how to do this. The same process applies to any software package you use within Windows.

You will need a floppy disk for some tasks in this section.

Hint:

Your computer needs an operating system in order to make it work. You will be using a version of Windows, e.g. Windows 98, or Windows Me (Millennium). Find out which one.

Information: Folders

So far you have saved your publications into a file store called **My Documents** or **My Work**. On a single standalone computer this will be on the hard disk (called **C: drive**). If you are working in a college you will probably be on a network (possibly **N: drive** but this may vary – check with your supervisor/tutor). As the number of publications and other files increases, it makes sense to organise your files into categories. This is done by creating folders and putting related files together so that you can find them easily later. (Saved publications are also known as files.) Folders should be given relevant names just as publications/files should. You are going to create folders using Windows.

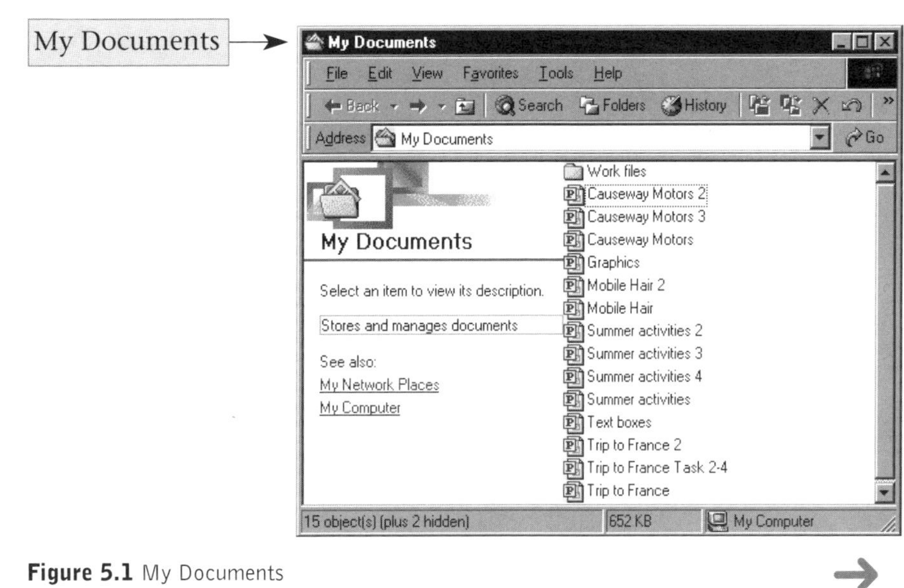

Figure 5.1 My Documents

→

If you have Publisher or any other program open, close them down now – this should take you back to the Windows desktop. You may see the My Documents or My Work folder already open in a window showing a list of your files. If so, this will look *similar* to Figure 5.1, though not necessarily the same, as it depends which version of Windows you are using. If you do not see this folder, locate the My Documents or My Work icon on your desktop – see Figure 5.2. Double click on this icon and the folder will open up.

Figure 5.2 My Documents icon

In the example in Figure 5.1 there is already one folder called Work files and several Publisher files. You are going to create two folders called **Tasks** and **Skills Practice**.

Task 5.1 Create folders

Method

1 Click on the **File** menu and select **New**. A side menu appears (Figure 5.3).

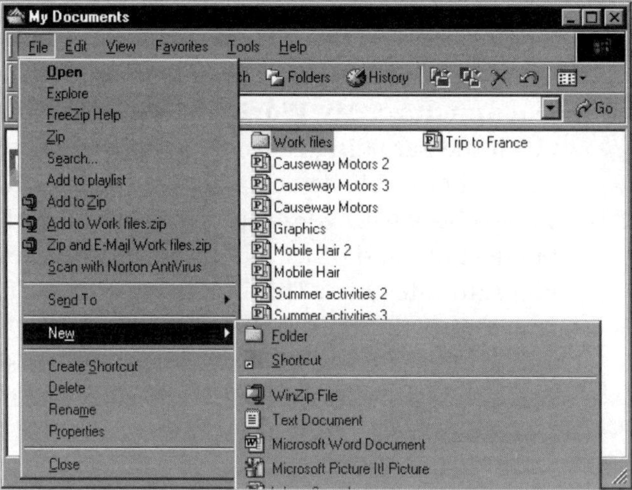

Figure 5.3 Create new folder

2 Click on **Folder**.
3 A new folder appears and the name **New Folder** is highlighted (Figure 5.4).
4 Key in the name **Tasks**.
5 Click off the folder to a blank area of the screen.
6 Repeat this process naming another new folder **Skills Practice**.

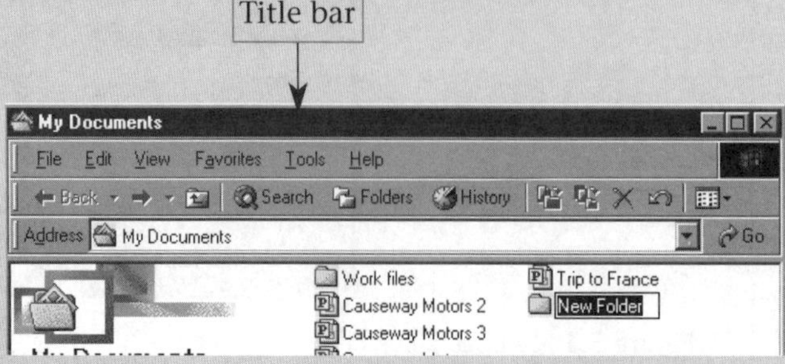

Figure 5.4 Name new folder

Information

You are now going to move files from one folder to another and to do this you are going to open the two new folders. You will end up with three folders open, **My Documents** at the top of the screen and **Tasks** and **Skills Practice** folders in the bottom left and right corners respectively.

Task 5.2 Open folders

Method

1. Position the pointer on the blue **My Documents** title bar (Figure 5.4). Press and drag to move it to the top of the screen.
2. Double click on the **Tasks** folder icon to open it.
3. Resize the **Tasks** folder window to make it smaller by positioning the pointer over the bottom right-hand corner. When the pointer changes to a double-headed arrow, drag gently towards the middle of the folder window to make it smaller.
4. Drag the **Tasks** folder title bar to move it to the bottom left corner of the screen.
5. Double click on the **Skills Practice** folder icon to open it.
6. Resize the **Skills Practice** folder window to make it smaller as before.
7. Drag the **Skills Practice** folder title bar to move it to the bottom right corner of the screen.
8. Click in each window in turn and watch the title bar turn blue indicating it is the selected window.

Task 5.3 Move files between folders

Method

1. Click in the **My Documents** window.
2. Position the mouse on **Causeway Motors** and holding the left button down, drag the file onto the **Skills Practice** folder and release. The file is moved.
3. Repeat for the other **Causeway Motors** files.
4. Move the **Trip to France** files into the **Tasks** folder.

Task 5.4 Delete a file

Method

1. Click on the **My Documents** folder.
2. Click on the file **Text frames**.
3. Press the **Delete** key on the keyboard.
4. Close each of the folder windows by clicking on the Close icon in the top right corner of each window.

Information

As well as reorganising files into folders, you can save them directly into folders when you create them.

Task 5.5 Save a publication into a folder

Method

1. Load Publisher and create a new blank publication.
2. Create a text box and key in the town/city of your birth, e.g. **London**.
3. Click on the **File** menu and choose **Save**. Save As dialogue box appears (Figure 5.5).
4. Double click on the **Tasks** folder. **Save in:** box now shows **Tasks** folder is open (Figure 5.6).
5. Key in an appropriate name, e.g. **London**, and click on **Save**.
6. Close the publication.

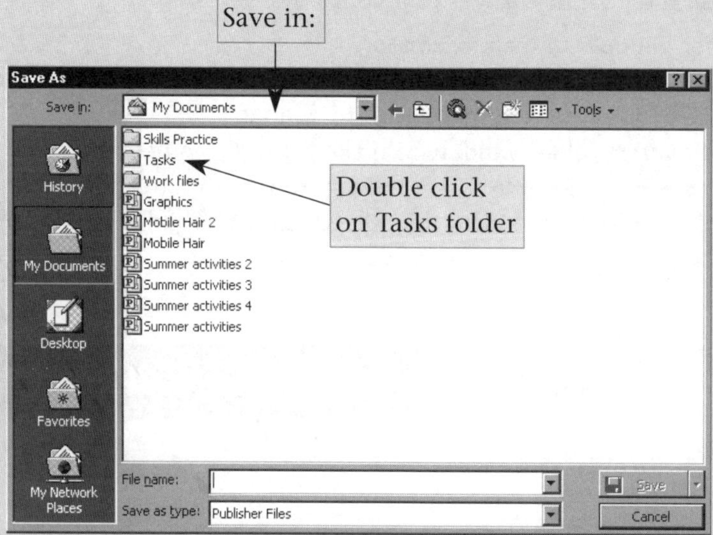

Figure 5.5 Save As dialogue box

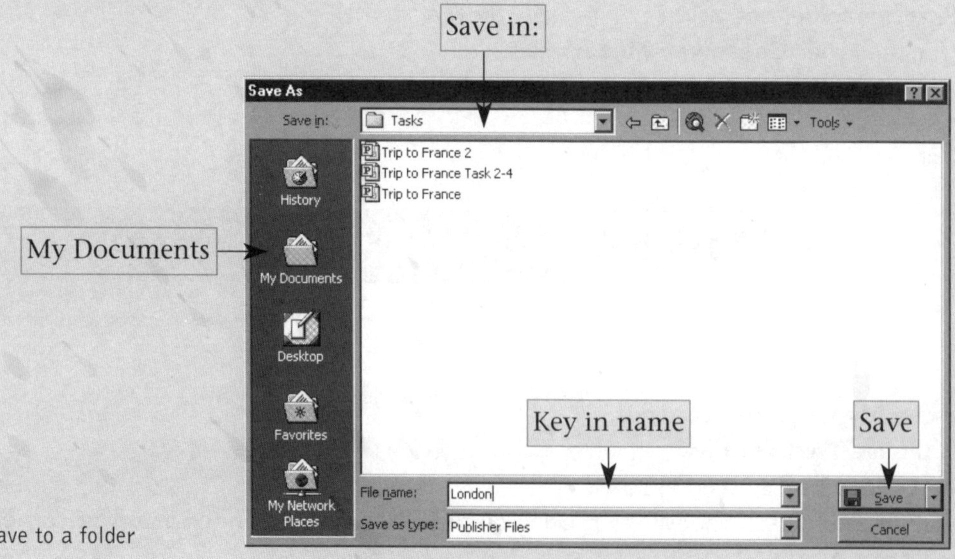

Figure 5.6 Save to a folder

Task 5.6 Save to another folder

Method

1. Create a new publication and create a text box. Key in the month of your birth, e.g. **April**.
2. Click on the **File** menu and select **Save**. **Save As** dialogue box opens as in Figure 5.5.
3. Notice how the Save in: box still reads **Tasks** as this was the folder you last used.
4. Click on **My Documents** in the left side bar (Figure 5.6). The Save in: box should now read **My Documents**.
5. Double click on **Skills Practice** folder. The Save in: box should now read **Skills Practice**.
6. Key in a suitable name, e.g. **April**.
7. Click on **Save**.

Hint:

When saving or opening files to and from different locations always start off in **My Documents** (click in the left side bar in the Save/Open dialogue box (Figure 5.6) if unsure where you are!

Information

Sometimes you might also want to save a file onto a floppy disk as a backup copy in case something happens to the original, or you may want to take the file elsewhere. You have already inserted a picture from the floppy disk drive, otherwise called **A: drive**.

Task 5.7 Save a file to a floppy disk

Method

1. Insert a floppy disk into the disk drive with the label uppermost and nearest to you.
2. Push it gently but firmly into the drive.
3. Using the same file, select **Save As** from the **File** menu.
4. Click on the down arrow alongside the **Save in**: box (Figure 5.7).

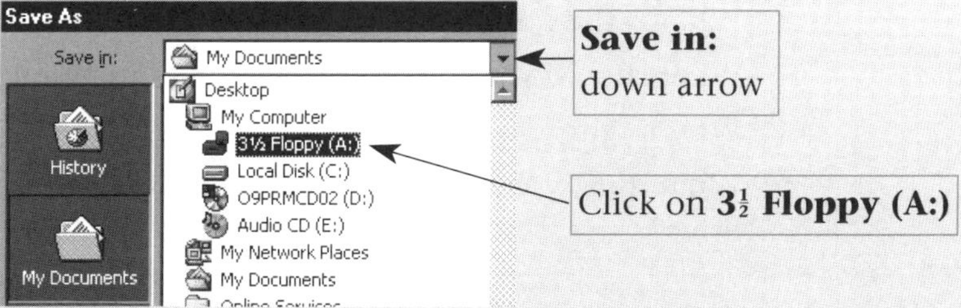

Figure 5.7 Select A: drive

5. Click on **3½ Floppy (A:)**.
6. Key in the filename you previously used, e.g. **April**, and click on **Save**. The disk drive light is on whilst the file is being saved.
7. Close the publication.
8. When the disk drive light goes out, push the small button which is usually directly below the drive and the disk is released. (Make sure you do not press the power button which may be nearby!)

You now have a copy of this publication on the floppy disk and in the Skills Practice folder.

Hint: Never take a floppy disk out while the disk drive light is on.

→ Practise your skills 1

1. Create a new publication and insert a picture of a computer.
2. Save the publication as **Computer** into **My Documents**.
3. Use **Save As** to save it into the **Skills Practice** folder.
4. Now use **Save As** to save it onto a floppy disk.
5. Close the publication.

→ Practise your skills 2

1. Create a folder called **Activities**.
2. Move all the files called **Summer Activities** (1, 2 and 3) into the new folder.

→ Practise your skills 3

1. Create a folder called **Hair**.
2. Move all the files called **Mobile Hair** (1 and 2) into the new folder.

→ Practise your skills 4

1. Open the publication called **Graphics** from **My Documents**.
2. Save it onto floppy disk.
3. Close the publication.
4. Delete it from My Documents.
5. Delete **Computer** from My Documents.

→ Check your knowledge

1. What is the difference between a folder and a directory?
2. What is the purpose of a folder?
3. What should you remember when naming a folder?
4. Why might you save a file onto a floppy disk?
5. What must you check for before removing a floppy disk from the drive?

Section 6 Page layout

You will learn to

- Identify common paper sizes
- Change page margins
- Create columns
- Place text and clip art into columns
- Change line spacing

Remember:

Remember paper orientation by thinking of a wide panoramic view for landscape and a tall upright portrait painting for portrait.

So far you have created publications on A4 and A5 paper using single text frames. In this section you will look at other paper sizes and work with text and images and divide the page into sections by using columns.

Information

Paper size

The standard paper size in use is **A4** (the size of pages in this book). This is based on International Standard (ISO) sizes where each size is half that of the next biggest size. Generally, all printers take A4 paper and most will handle smaller sizes. For this book you will only use A4 and A5 but you should be aware of all four of the paper sizes below.

You have already learnt about paper orientation in Section 1.

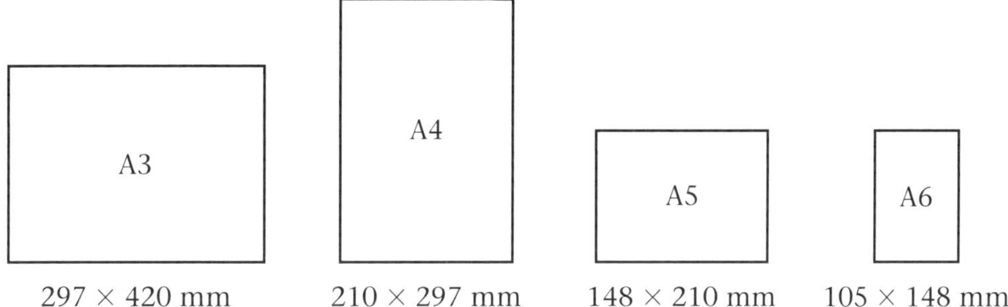

297 × 420 mm 210 × 297 mm 148 × 210 mm 105 × 148 mm

Changing page margins

Publisher margins are merely guides to assist you in placing objects on the page, and whilst you can ignore them, anything placed too close to the edge of the page may not print. Using the margin guides will ensure your pages are balanced. Margin size will depend on the publication and the size of the paper. A5, for example, will usually have smaller margins than A4.

Using columns

A page can be divided into columns to give interest to the page or make it easier to read. It might also improve the layout by splitting it into sections rather than one big 'chunk'. Another reason why columns are used is to divide the page for the creation of folding leaflets, the fold being made between columns. You are going to create a publication comprising two columns with a heading spread across the top.

Task 6.1 Change layout guides to set margins and columns

Method

1 Load Publisher if not already loaded and open a new publication.
2 Select **Print Setup** from the **File** menu and change the paper size to A5 landscape. Notice how big the margins appear to be in relation to the size of the page.

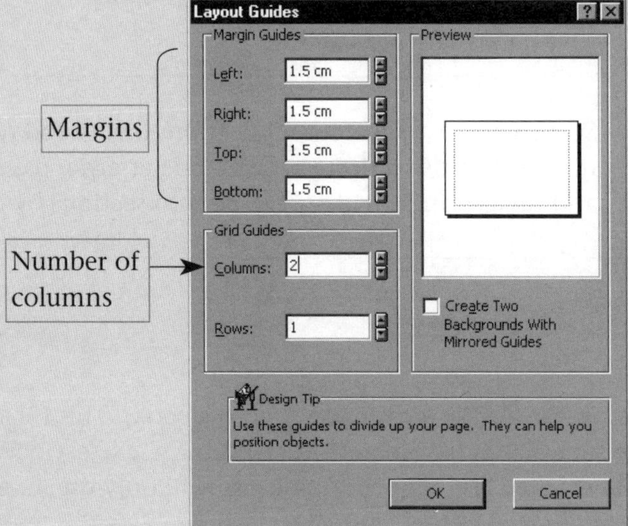

Figure 6.1 Change layout guides

3 Click the **Arrange** menu and select **Layout Guides**. Dialogue box appears (Figure 6.1).
4 Click in the **Left** margin box and key in **1.5**.
5 Repeat for the **Right** margin and then the **Top** and **Bottom**.
6 Click in the **Columns** box and key in **2**.
7 Click **OK**.

The page margins can be seen in pink and the column guides are blue.

Information: The gutter

The gap between the columns is 0.5 cm (0.25″) and is called the **gutter**. (This term is also used to refer to the margins in the middle of a two-page spread.)

Task 6.2 Create a heading across the columns

Method

1 Select the Text Frame tool and draw a text frame that stretches from the blue column guide on the left right across to the guide on the right side of the page.
2 Key in the heading **VILLAGE FUN DAY**.
3 Centre the heading and embolden it.
4 Change it to a sans serif font of your choice and increase the size to around 36.

Task 6.3 Place text into columns

Method

1. Create a text frame below the heading in the top half of the left column (between the blue column guides) and key in the following text:

   Saturday July 27th
   At the Memorial Field
   Starting at 1.30 pm
   Prize Draw at 4 pm

2. Save the publication as **Village Fun Day**.
3. Change the text size to **18**. Enlarge the text frame if necessary.
4. Change the text to a sans serif font of your choice.
5. Centre all the text.
6. Create a text frame in the bottom half of the right column and key in the following:

   Hot air balloon rides
   Barbeque
   Pony rides
   Raffle
   Sideshows
   And much more ...

7. Centre this text and change the font and size to the same used in the left column. Enlarge the text frame if necessary but keep within the margins.
8. Spellcheck, proofread and save the publication.

Hint: Pull the top handle of the text box upwards to prevent text going below the bottom margin.

Information: Line spacing

Publisher automatically leaves a small space between lines when you start a new line or press Enter. Sometimes you may want to vary this according to the space you have available. See Figure 6.2.

Here there are 2 spaces between lines - usually known as double line spacing. There is one extra line space between each line of text.

In this example thare are 1.5 spaces between lines of text. This is often referred to as one and a half line spacing.

Figure 6.2 Line spacing

Task 6.4 Change line spacing

Method

1. Highlight the text in the left-hand column.
2. Click on the **Format** menu and choose **Line spacing**.

Hint:

The space will vary according to the size of the font.

Hint:

You can also change line spacing by highlighting text and holding down the Ctrl key to the left of the spacebar and pressing 1 (Ctrl + 1) for single spacing, Ctrl + 2 for double, Ctrl + 5 for one and a half.

3 Click into the box alongside **Between lines** (Figure 6.3) and key in **2**. Click **OK**.

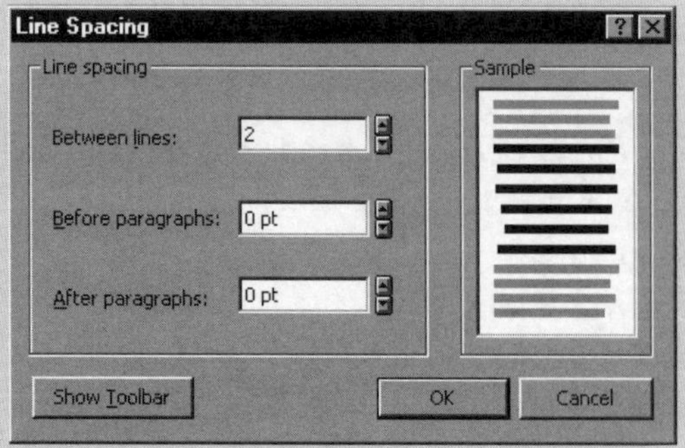

Figure 6.3 Choose line spacing

4 Adjust the text frame if necessary to show all the text.
5 Highlight the text in the right-hand column and change the line spacing to **1.5**.
6 Adjust the size of the text frame if necessary.
7 Place an image of a hot air balloon above the text frame on the right-hand side.
8 Place a suitable image below the text frame on the left.
9 Save the publication, print and close.

Task 6.5 Change line spacing following a paragraph

It is also possible to vary the space following a paragraph if you require more space or if you need to insert an image, for example.

Hint:

You can also simply press Enter between lines to create this space.

Method

1 Open a new publication and draw a text frame.
2 Key in your name and press **Enter**.
3 Key in the name of your home town.
4 Click on the line displaying your name.
5 Select **Line spacing** from the **Format** menu (see Figure 6.3).
6 Key in 120 in the box alongside **After paragraphs** and click **OK**.

NOTE: This measurement is in point size not line spaces. 30 points gives a space of about 1 cm.

7 Now insert a clip art image in the space between the lines.
8 Experiment with the spacing between paragraphs.
9 Close the publication without saving.

→ Practise your skills 1

1. Create a new folder and call it **Quarryfields**.
2. Open a new blank publication and change the print setup to A5 landscape.
3. Change the margins to 1 cm all round and number of columns to 2 with a gutter of 0.5 cm (0.25″). (This is the default gutter.)
4. Create a text frame across the columns and key in the heading **QUARRYFIELDS COLLEGE**.
5. Format the text to Arial, size 36, embolden and centre.
6. Create a text frame in the first column and key in:

   City & Guilds
   e-Quals
   Level 1
   Starting next month
   For information call in now
   Level 2 also available
7. Change the text to Arial, size 18, double line (2) spacing.
8. Embolden the first two lines and increase their size to 20.
9. Save the publication as **e-Quals** into the **Quarryfields** folder.
10. Create a text frame in the second column and key in:
    IT Principles
    Word Processing
    Spreadsheets
    Databases
    Using the Internet
    Presentation Graphics
    E-Mail
    Desktop Publishing
11. Format the text to Arial, size 18, 1.5 line spacing and aligned to the right.
12. Change the text to blue throughout.
13. Insert a picture of a person using a computer between the 2 columns.
14. Spellcheck and proofread.
15. Save, print and close.

→ Practise your skills 2

1. Open a new blank publication and set the print setup as A4 landscape.
2. Divide the page into 3 columns with a gutter of 0.5 cm (0.25″). (This is the default gutter.)
3. Create a text frame across the columns and key in the heading **QUARRYFIELDS COLLEGE.**
4. Format the text to Arial, size 48, embolden and centre.
5. Create a text frame in the first column and key in:

   Courses for the Autumn
   Enrolling NOW
   Call in any time between 9 am and 7 pm
   Vocational Courses
   Leisure Courses
6. Underline the text **Enrolling NOW**.

7 Save the publication as **Autumn courses** into the **Quarryfields** folder.

8 Format the text in the first column to Arial, size 20. Resize the text frame if necessary.

9 Create a text frame in the middle column and key in:

VOCATIONAL COURSES
Information Technology
Business
Health and Social Care
Media Studies
Catering
And many more . . .

10 Format this text to Arial, size 18 and centre it. Embolden the first line only. Resize the text frame if necessary.

11 Create a text frame in the third column and key in:

LEISURE COURSES
Art
Cookery
Sports
Yoga
Flower Arranging
And many more . . .

12 Format this text to Arial, size 18 and centre it. Embolden the first line only. Resize the text frame if necessary.

13 Change the text in all columns to double (2) line spacing.

14 Change the text to blue throughout.

15 Move the middle text frame to the bottom of the column.

16 Place a suitable image below the first and third columns (e.g. search for autumn and cook) and above the second column (e.g. computer).

17 Spellcheck and proofread.

18 Save, print and close.

→ Check your knowledge

1 What paper size and orientation are the pages of this book?

2 What is the relationship between the sizes of A3, A4, A5 and A6?

3 What is a gutter?

4 Why might you use columns?

5 What is double line spacing?

Consolidation 2

1 Create a new folder in My Work and call it **Consolidation**.

2 Create a new A4 blank publication and set up the page as follows:

Orientation	Landscape
Left Margin	2 cm (0.75″)
Right Margin	2 cm (0.75″)
Top Margin	2 cm (0.75″)
Bottom Margin	2 cm (0.75″)
Columns	3
Gutter	0.5 cm (0.25″) (this is the default)

3 Save the publication as **Pepe's Pizza Palace** into the **Consolidation** folder.

4 Key in text as shown in the sketch below:

Pepe's Pizza Palace

clipart

13 Market Place
Pitford
Tel 0987 736736

Take-away Menu

Pizzas

Original Cheese
Pepperoni
Spicy Chilli
Vegetarian
Chicken Supreme
Tropical Surprise
Sausage and bacon

clipart

clipart

Extras

Garlic Bread
Potato Wedges
French Fries
Soft Drinks
Banoffee Pie

Remember:

When selecting a colour by name, rest the pointer over the colour and its name appears.

5 Main heading should be in bold, size 48, sans serif font, centred and light orange.

6 Text in first column should be size 24, same font as heading, centred and coloured green.

7 Text in middle column should be size 20, same font, centred and coloured light orange.

8 Text in third column should be size 20, same font, centred and coloured green.

9 Headings in the middle and third column should be bold with a line spacing after the heading only, of 25 points.

10 Insert clip art where indicated.

11 Spellcheck and proofread.

12 Save, print and close.

Section 7 Further formatting

You will learn to

- Change character spacing
- Change to upper case
- Apply superscript and subscript
- Apply fill style to text frames and clip art
- Add a border to text frames and clip art
- Apply and change text wrap settings

In this section you will find out more about formatting your publication by changing the appearance of text – characters and text frames – as well as clip art, and the way text wraps around it.

Information: Character spacing

It is possible to adjust the spacing between characters (or letters) in order to make them closer together or further apart. The correct term for this is **tracking**. You may want to do this to add variety to your layout or in order to fit text into a specific space.

Task 7.1 Change character spacing

Method

1 Open the publication **Village Fun Day** from **My Documents**.
2 Highlight the main heading and select **Character spacing** from the **Format** menu (Figure 7.1).
3 Click on the drop down arrow beside **Normal** and select **Very Tight**. Click **OK**. Notice the effect as the characters move closer together.
4 With the text still highlighted, repeat this process selecting **Loose**. Notice the effect.
5 Finally, with the text still highlighted, repeat this process and select **Very Loose**.
6 Save the publication as **Village Fun Day 2**.

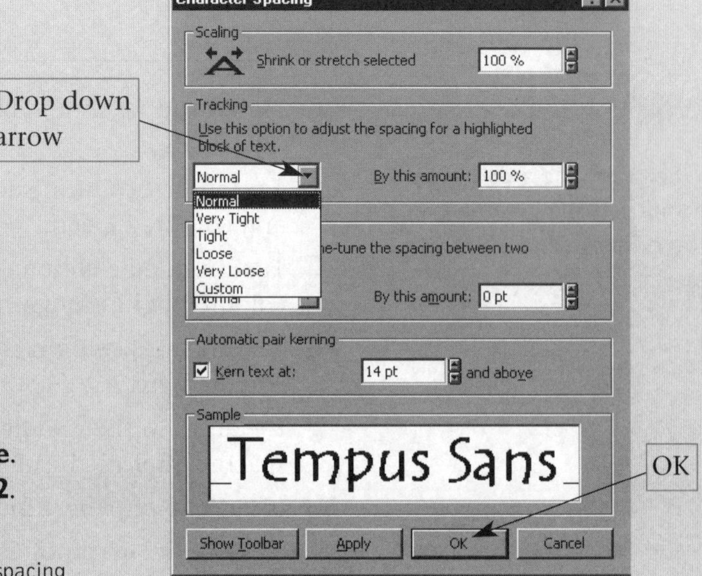

Figure 7.1 Character spacing

Information: Upper case format

When you have keyed in text it is possible to change it to display all capital letters (upper case) without keying it in again.

Task 7.2 Change to upper case

Method

1. Highlight the text **Starting at 1.30 pm** and select **Font** from the **Format** menu.
2. Click on **All caps** (Figure 7.2) – a tick appears. Click **OK**.
3. Highlight the text **And much more ...** and repeat this process.
4. Save the publication.

You can always change the text back to its previous format by clicking **Undo** straight away.

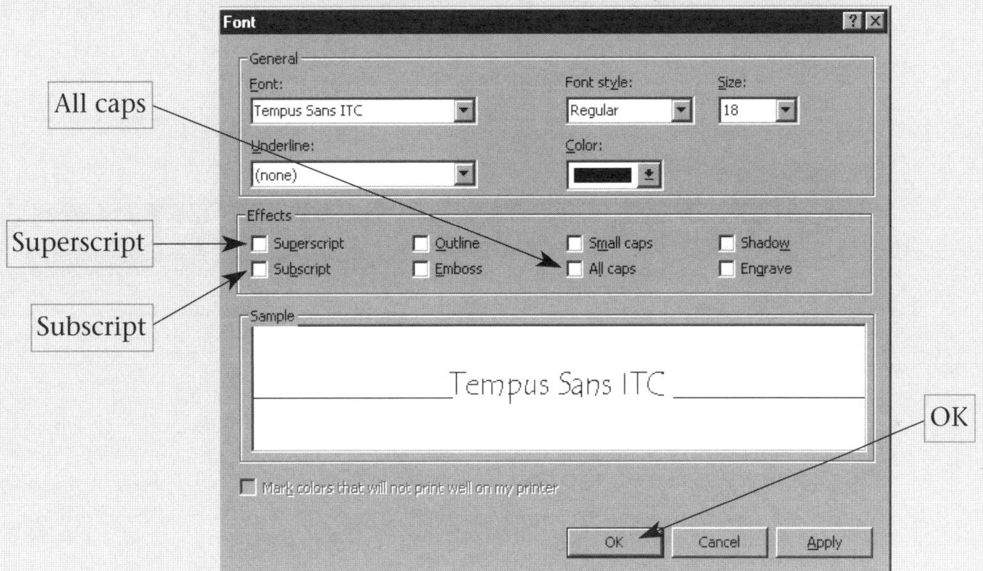

Figure 7.2 Change to upper case

Information: Subscript and superscript

Subscript characters are small characters that appear just below the characters around it, e.g. H_20. Superscript characters are raised just above, e.g. 10°C.

Task 7.3 Apply superscript

Method

1. Highlight the characters **th** in **Saturday July 27th** and select **Font** from the **Format** menu.
2. Click on **Superscript** (See Figure 7.2) – a tick appears. Click **OK**.
3. Save the publication.

Applying subscript is exactly the same process, but select **Subscript** instead.

Information: Text frame fill styles

The default text frame fill colour is white. It is possible to fill a text frame with a colour or with No fill. No fill means that it is transparent as opposed to being white – both actually look the same unless there is an object, such as clip art behind the text. If the text fill is white, the clip art will not show, whereas if No fill is applied it will show through. A fill is sometimes known as a background.

Task 7.4 Apply fill style to text frames

Method

1. Using the same publication click in the main heading to select the text frame.
2. Click on the **Fill Color** button and select a pale colour, e.g. pale blue.
3. Click in the text box in the left column and repeat the process selecting the same colour.
4. Repeat for the second column.
5. Save the publication.

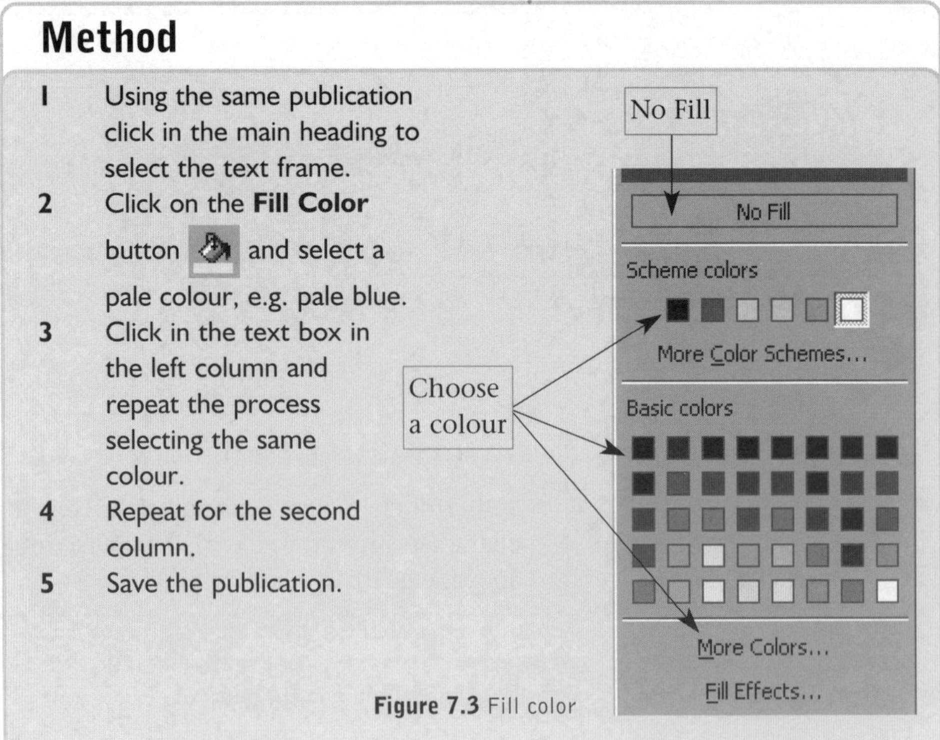

Figure 7.3 Fill color

Information

Clip art images can also have their background fill changed.

Task 7.5 Apply fill to clip art

Remember:

The Formatting toolbar changes depending on the object you are working with, e.g. text or clip art.

Method

1 Select one of the clip art images and click on the **Fill color** button . It is the same button as used in the previous task but this time will be in a different position on the **Object Formatting** toolbar.
2 Select a fill colour.
3 Repeat for the second image.
4 Now change both clip art images to a **No fill** style (Figure 7.3).
5 Save the publication.

Information

Another formatting technique is to add lines or borders to the edge of text frames and other objects such as clip art.

Task 7.6 Add a border to a text frame and clip art

Hint:

You can also click on More Styles for more choice.

Method

1 Using the same publication, click on the text frame of the main heading.
2 Click on the **Line/Border style** button and choose a line style. (Hairline is a very fine line.) You may need to adjust the depth of the text frame to accommodate the border.

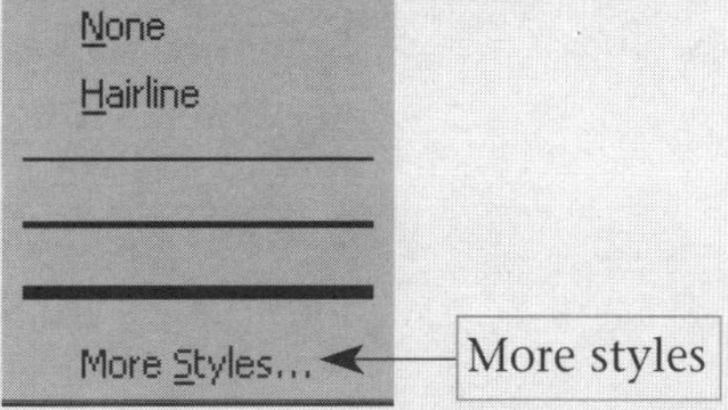

Figure 7.4 Line/Border style

3 Click on one of the clip art images and repeat this process. Note that the same button is used but it will be in a different position on the **Object Formatting** toolbar.
4 Click on the **Line color** button and choose a colour as you did for the fill colour above.
5 Experiment with the different styles and colours and note the effects achieved.
6 Proofread and when you are satisfied, save the publication, print and close.

Hint:

Too many lines and borders do not necessarily make a good display.

Information

Proofreading is not just about checking that text is accurate. When you are using graphics such as clip art, other images and shapes, it is also about checking that they are adjusted in size, number and positioned for a pleasing effect. Sometimes a slight adjustment can make all the difference.

Information: Text wrap settings

You have previously applied text wrap to a text frame so that the text wraps around an image placed on it. It is also possible to apply text wrap to fit around the shape of the object.

Task 7.7 Apply and change text wrap settings

Method

Hint:

If the text does not move away from the image, click on the **Text Frame Properties** button 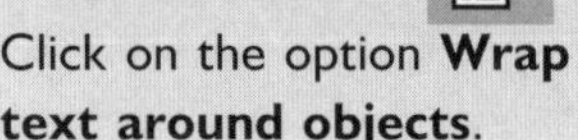. Click on the option **Wrap text around objects**.

1. Open the publication **e-Quals** from the **Quarryfields** folder.
2. Using the **Clip Gallery** tool, draw a frame in the bottom right corner over the text. The text should move out of the way as text wrap is applied to the text frame by default (Figure 7.5). Beware – some text may be moved into text overflow.

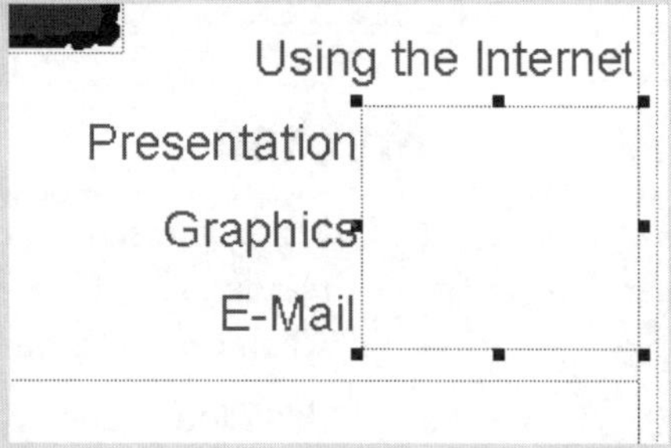

Figure 7.5 Draw clip art frame

3. Search for clip art on the keyword **computer keyboard**. Select an image that is *not* completely rectangular and insert. Notice how the text wraps around in a rectangular shape.
4. Click on the image if not already selected and click on **Wrap text to picture** button on the Object Formatting toolbar (Figure 7.6). Notice how the boundary around the image now follows its shape and the text wrap follows it too.

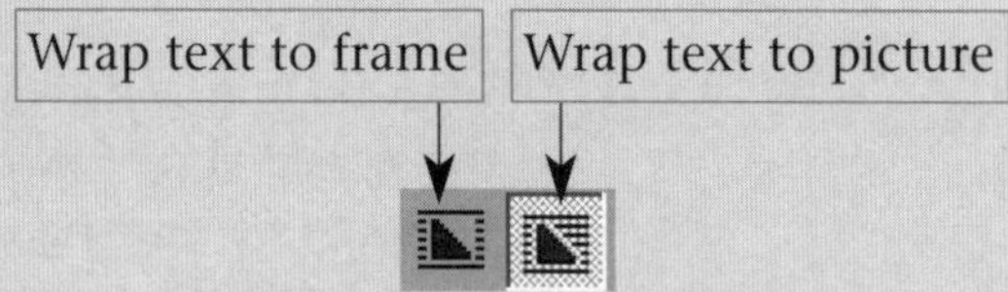

Figure 7.6 Wrap text

5. Click on the **Wrap text to frame** button and notice how the text wrap reverts back to a rectangular shape.
6. Now click **Wrap text to picture** again.
7. Make sure all the text is still displayed.
8. Save the publication as **e-Quals 2** and print. Close the publication.

Hint:

You may need to adjust the position of the image for a pleasing result.

Remember:

When opening a file from a different folder, click on My Documents in the side bar of the Open dialogue box to move back to My Documents first.

Hint:

When selecting a colour by name, rest the pointer over the colour and its name appears.

→ Practise your skills 1

1. Open the publication **Pepe's Pizza Palace** from the **Consolidation** folder.
2. Change the character spacing of the main heading to **Very Loose**.
3. Change the heading to upper case (**All caps**).
4. Change the headings of the second and third columns to upper case.
5. Add a border to the main heading and the other three text frames.
6. Change the heading text frame fill to gold.
7. Change the remaining three text frames to light yellow.
8. Change the address to **13^{a}** making the 'a' superscript.
9. Save the publication with the new name **Pepe's Pizza Palace 2** into the **Consolidation** folder and print. Close the publication.

Remember:

When resizing clip art, make sure you use a corner handle, not a side handle, to keep it in proportion.

→ Practise your skills 2

1. Open the publication **Mobile Hair 2** from the **Hair** folder.
2. Change the heading to upper case and **Very loose** character spacing.
3. Change the list of four services starting **Cuts ...** to upper case and **Loose** character spacing.
4. Align the last four lines to the right. (The last line already is.)
5. Insert a suitable clip art image in the bottom right corner of the page (search for **hairdresser** or **scissors**) and apply **Wrap text to picture**.
6. Enlarge the clip art in height and adjust the position and size for a pleasing effect.
7. Change the text frame fill to light turquoise.
8. Add a border to the text frame and change the colour to turquoise.
9. Proofread, making sure all the text is displayed, that the border does not touch the image and you are satisfied with the final result.
10. Save as **Mobile Hair 3** into the **Hair** folder and print.
11. Save a copy of the file onto floppy disk and close.

→ Check your knowledge

1. What does **tracking** mean?
2. What is meant by the terms **subscript** and **superscript**?
3. What is meant by **No fill**?
4. What does clicking on the **Wrap text to picture** button do?
5. How can you change text already keyed in to upper case?

Section 8 The DTP environment

You will learn to

- Describe the hardware and software used for desktop publishing
- Check memory (RAM) and storage space

In this section you will find out about the hardware and software associated with desktop publishing. Hardware, as you may already know, is the equipment you are working with, whilst software means the applications programs you use, such as Publisher.

Information: Hardware and software

Hardware

So far you have used the following:

- the **keyboard** to enter text
- the **mouse** to select buttons and menus, highlight text, move objects, etc.
- the **monitor** or **VDU** (Visual Display Unit) to view your work
- the **hard disk** to store your work (C: drive on a single standalone computer and possibly N: drive if you are using a network)
- a **floppy disk** to store your work and to obtain images
- a **CD-ROM** to obtain stored images
- a **printer** to print your work.

Another item of hardware often used when desktop publishing is a **scanner**. It gives you the ability to insert any image into your work. If you place a picture, photograph or drawing on the flat glass surface, the scanning software scans the image and converts it to a **bitmap** image – and a file which you can save. Scanning software often has the ability to scan text and convert it into a text file which you can insert into your publications and both edit and format. This saves a lot of time because you do not have to key it all in. This process is called **Optical Character Recognition** or **OCR**.

Figure 8.1 Scanner

Software

Apart from your desktop publishing software and the OCR software mentioned above, the following applications software may also be used for creating elements of a DTP publication:

- **Text editing** software – used to create simple, plain text to insert into a publication.
- **Word processing** software – as for text editing but is more sophisticated and any formatting, e.g. fonts, bold etc., may be retained when inserted into a publication.
- **Graphics** software – used to create images or to change them before inserting them into a publication.

Information: RAM memory

When working with DTP software, you are working with a number of graphical objects and constantly moving them around. This takes up a lot of the computer's memory, more so than straightforward word processing of text. This memory is called **RAM** (**Random Access Memory**) and your work is held in this memory until you save it. If you do not save and your computer freezes or is switched off, your work is lost. If you have a number of publications or other files open and perhaps other programs as well, they are taking up space in the RAM too. Your computer will work slower the more you have open and could grind to a halt resulting in you losing your work. You can check the amount of RAM available before you start work and you may be required to do this for your assignment.

Task 8.1 Check available RAM

If Publisher is still open you can close it altogether or minimise it, which leaves Publisher running but 'shrinks' it down into the taskbar at the bottom of the screen.

Method

1 Click on the **Minimise** button in the top right corner of the window (Figure 8.2). This should take you back to the Windows desktop. If not, close down or minimise any other programs or files you have open. Notice how Publisher still appears in the taskbar at the bottom of the screen.

Figure 8.2 Minimise

Figure 8.3 My Computer

2 Locate the **My Computer** icon (Figure 8.3) on the desktop, possibly in the top left corner.

3 Click the right mouse button on **My Computer** and select **Properties**.

4 Click on the **Performance** tab (Figure 8.4). Note the amount of free space.

5 Close the **System Properties** window by clicking on the X in the top right corner to close it.

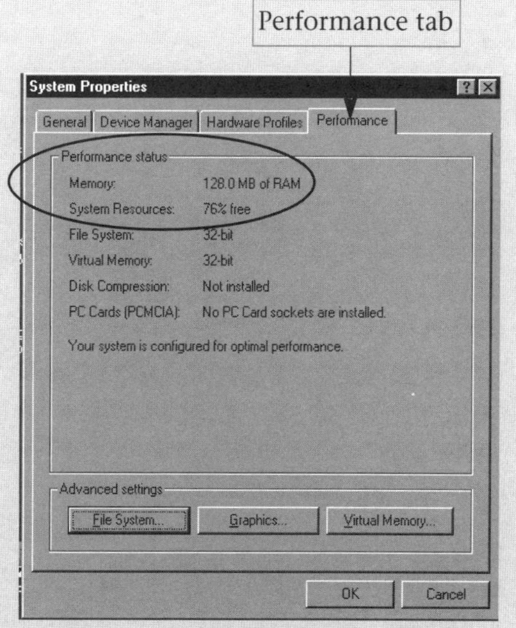

Figure 8.4 Check RAM

Information

You can see that the RAM memory on the computer in Figure 8.4 is 128 MB and 76% is currently free, so there is plenty of RAM available. If you had as little as 30% free, you might well have difficulty in working and should close down any unnecessary files and applications and then check it again.

Information: Storage space

Just as desktop publishing files use a lot of RAM, the saved files or publications also take up storage space. On a single computer at home, your work is saved on C: drive. In a college, it might be saved on N: drive. You may of course save to a floppy disk (A: drive) or even onto CD if you have a CD Writer. In order to be sure you have sufficient storage space for your files you can check the available space.

Task 8.2 Check storage space

Method

1. Minimise Publisher or any other programs or files.
2. Double click on the **My Computer** icon. The window opens (Figure 8.5). Your window may look different to this one with the icons shown one below the other. (You may even see a pie chart indicating the space available.)
3. To check the C: drive, right click on the **Local Disk (C:)** icon. See Figure 8.6. Note the free space.

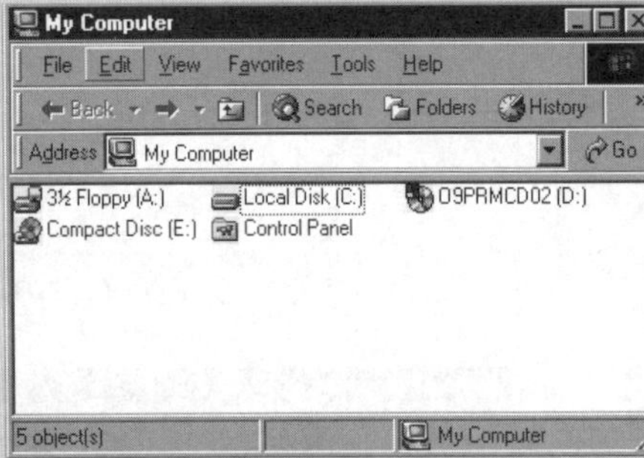

Figure 8.5 Check storage

4. Close both the windows above.
5. To return to Publisher, click on Publisher in the taskbar at the bottom of the window.

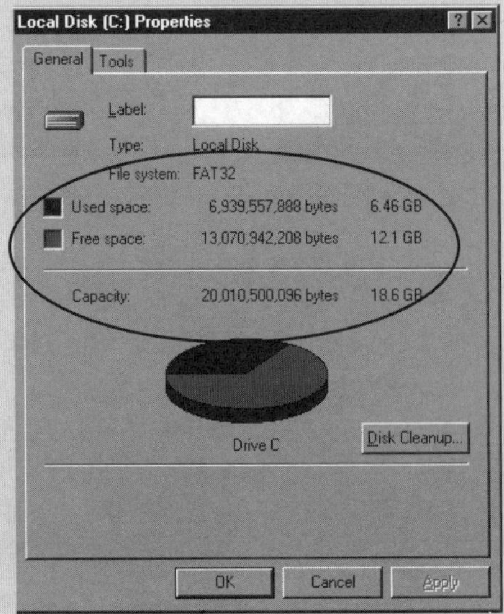

Figure 8.6 Available memory

Hint:

To check any other drive, right click on the appropriate icon.

Information

You can see the total capacity is 18.6 GB with 12.1 GB free, so there is a huge amount of space available.

→ Practise your skills 1

1. Create a new Publisher publication – A4 landscape.
2. Create a text frame in the centre and key in **DTP** in font size **48**.
3. Search for and place clip art images of the hardware items listed in the Hardware section above, as well as a scanner, and place them around the edge of the page in a rough circle. (You may not find them all.)
4. Create a small separate text frame for each and key in the name of each item. Shade each text frame in grey 25% (light grey).
5. Centre the text in each frame, format as you wish and add a border.
6. Adjust all the elements until you are satisfied.
7. Spellcheck and proofread.
8. Save as **DTP** into the **Skills Practice** folder, print and close.

→ Practise your skills 2

1. Check, and make a note of, the amount of memory (RAM) on your system and how much is free.
2. Check, and make a note of, the amount of storage space on your system and how much is free.
3. Create a new A5 portrait publication.
4. Create a text frame and key in the information you have written down.
5. Format and arrange it as you wish.
6. Create a text frame just below the margin in the bottom right corner of the page and key in the date. (Make sure your name is also included on the page as always.)
7. Save as **Memory and storage** into the **Skills Practice** folder, print and close.

→ Check your knowledge

1. Describe two uses for a scanner.
2. Give one advantage of using a scanner.
3. What does RAM stand for?
4. Why might you check available memory (RAM) and storage space before creating DTP files?
5. Name three other applications software packages that are commonly used for creating elements of a DTP publication..

Section 9 Further page layout and copy and paste

You will learn to

- Change the gutter between columns
- Use copy and paste on text and clip art

In this section you will find out how to change the page layout by altering the gutter width between columns. You will also copy text frames, text and clip art.

Information: Changing the gutter

So far, when working with columns, you have used the default gutter of 0.5 cm (0.25″). In order to set a gutter of your choice you must use ruler guides. If the rulers across the top of the window and down the left side are not visible, select **Rulers** from the **View** menu. Note the measurements across the top ruler from 0 to 21 cm, making the midpoint 10.5 cm on A4 portrait. You are now going to make the gutter 1 cm so it will be positioned from 10 to 11 cm on the ruler. Ruler guides appear as green lines onscreen.

Remember:

The gutter is the space between columns.

Task 9.1 Change the gutter

Hint:

It is possible to set a gutter if you divide a large text frame into columns using Text Properties, but this is only suitable for text that snakes down one column and continues into the next.

Method

1. Open a new blank publication. Set it up as A4 portrait, with margins of 2 cm all round.
2. Hold the Shift key down and position the mouse on the vertical ruler on the left of the window. The pointer changes to the Adjust pointer ADJUST
3. Drag the Adjust pointer to 10 cm on the horizontal ruler scale (at the top of the screen) and release.
4. Repeat this process positioning the second guide at 11 cm.
5. Create a text box across the top of the two columns from margin to margin and key in **Health and Safety**.
6. Change the font to a sans serif font, size 48, centred and bold.
7. Save the publication as **Health and Safety** into the **Tasks** folder.
8. Create a text frame in the left column and key in the following:

It is important that anyone working with computers is aware of the importance of health and safety issues.

When operating a computer the height of the chair should be adjustable as should the tilt of the back of the chair. Knees should fit comfortably under the desk.

There should be sufficient working space to allow for papers on the desk. Gangways between desks should be kept clear.

Monitors should be capable of swivelling to suit the user and tilting up and down. Glare from windows and light should be avoided and the user should adjust the brightness to suit.

Keyboards should be positioned towards the front of the desk and have the ability to be tilted or flat. Wrists should be straight not bent and wrist rests can be made available.

Sufficient lighting is necessary and blinds should be available at windows to avoid glare. Temperature should ideally be around 20° C. Heat can build up very quickly around computer equipment.

9 Spellcheck, proofread and save.

Remember:

Use a superscript for the degrees symbol in 20° C.

Information: Copy and paste a text frame

You have previously moved text frames. You are now going to **copy** a text frame and **paste** it elsewhere. When you copy an object such as a text frame, it is held in an area of memory called the **clipboard**. You can then paste it out and move it to the required position.

Task 9.2 Copy and paste a text frame

Method

1 Click on the main heading text frame to select.
2 Click on the **Copy** button on the Standard toolbar (Figure 9.1).

Figure 9.1 Cut, copy and paste

3 Click on **Paste**. A copy of the heading appears almost on top of the original. Move it down to the bottom of the page.
4 Save the publication.

Remember:

Position the pointer on the edge of a text frame for the **Move** symbol to appear.

Task 9.3 Copy and paste text

You are now going to copy the first paragraph and paste it into a new text frame.

Method

1 Highlight the text in the first paragraph beginning **It is important ...**
2 Click on the **Copy** button.
3 In the right-hand column, create a text frame big enough to hold the first paragraph and with the cursor flashing inside it, click on **Paste**.
4 Move this text frame down to the bottom of the second column.
5 Save the publication.

Task 9.4 Cut and paste text (Move)

You are now going to **cut** text out from the first text frame and **paste** it into another. This is also known as **moving** text.

Method

1. Create a new text box in the right-hand column, key in **Seating** as a heading and press **Enter** twice to leave a clear line space.
2. Highlight the paragraph beginning **When operating …** and click on **Cut**.
3. Click into the new text frame below the heading (ensuring you leave the line space clear) and click on **Paste**.
4. Repeat this process creating 4 more separate text frames with headings for **Space**, **Monitors**, **Keyboards**, **Lighting and Heating**. If you run out of space, use the left-hand column as well, or the scratch area off the page.
5. Cut and paste the appropriate paragraph into each.
6. Change the size of the text (except main heading) to **12** with the paragraph headings made **bold**.
7. Adjust the size of the text frames to fit the text.
8. Arrange the frames leaving gaps to place some clip art images.
9. Insert one clip art image of a computer and one of somebody working at a computer – you will add more in the next task.
10. Proofread, save and print.

Task 9.5 Copy clip art

You have already moved clip art on several occasions. Just as you can copy text and text frames, you can also copy clip art.

Method

1. Click on one of the clip art images to select it and then click on **Copy**.
2. Click on **Paste**. The copy appears almost on top of the original. Move it off the page on to the scratch area.
3. Click on **Paste** again. A further copy appears. Move it off the page.
4. Click on the second image you inserted and click on **Copy**.
5. Click on **Paste** and move it off the page.
6. Click on **Paste** once more. A further copy should appear. Move it off the page.
7. Position the images as you think fit, resizing them as required.
8. Proofread, making sure the text is all visible and readable, save and print.

→ Practise your skills 1

In this task you are going to change the page setup and gutter, and copy and paste the text from the small text frames into two larger text frames.

1. Using the same **Health and Safety** publication, delete the copied heading across the bottom of the page.
2. Delete one of the duplicated text frames starting **It is important …**
3. Delete all the clip art leaving one image.

Remember:

To delete a text frame, click on it to select and choose **Delete Object** from the **Edit** menu.

Remember:

Hold the Shift key down to move a ruler guide.

Remember:

Save as you work.

4. Change the page setup to landscape.
5. Adjust the ruler guides to make the gutter **2 cm** – this will put them at just under **14** cm and just under **16** cm on the scale.
6. Save as **Health and Safety 2** into the **Skills Practice** folder.
7. Move the **Health and Safety** heading to the bottom of the page and resize to fit the width of the page.
8. Position the text frame starting **It is important . . .** at the top of the left column and move all the others out of the way on to the scratch area.
9. Stretch this text frame across the column and make it deeper by pulling down the bottom handle ready to paste text into it.
10. Highlight the text in the **Lighting and Heating** text frame and click on **Cut**.
11. Position the cursor at the end of the text in the left column and press Enter twice. Click on **Paste**.
12. Repeat this process (steps 10 and 11) with the **Space** text.
13. Delete any empty text frames.
14. Place the **Seating** text frame at the top of the right column, stretch it across the column and make it deeper.
15. **Cut** and **paste** the **Monitors** text and the **Keyboards** text into this frame in the same way as before.
16. Delete any empty text frames.
17. Enlarge the text in the two text frames to **14** with the headings at size **16**.
18. Adjust the size of the text frames to fit the text.
19. Copy and paste the clip art image **four** times and position them across the empty space.
20. Fill all three text frames with light grey (grey 25%).
21. Proofread, save, print and close.

→ Check your knowledge

1. What is the clipboard?
2. What is the difference between copy and paste and cut and paste?
3. What guides do you use to change the gutter manually?

Section 10 Manipulating graphic objects

You will learn to

- Crop, rotate and flip objects
- Use Shape tools
- Layer objects

You have already used graphic objects in the form of clip art. In this section you will work with other graphic objects such as lines and shapes. Much of what you have learnt to do with text frames and clip art applies here and you will also learn some new techniques. You will also find out about placing objects in layers, i.e. on top of each other.

Information

The Object toolbar changes depending on the object you have selected. Many of the tools are the same for every object.

Task 10.1 Crop an image

You are already familiar with many of the tools on the Object toolbar for images. Cropping means to 'cover over' part of an image so it does not show. You can 'uncrop' if you wish.

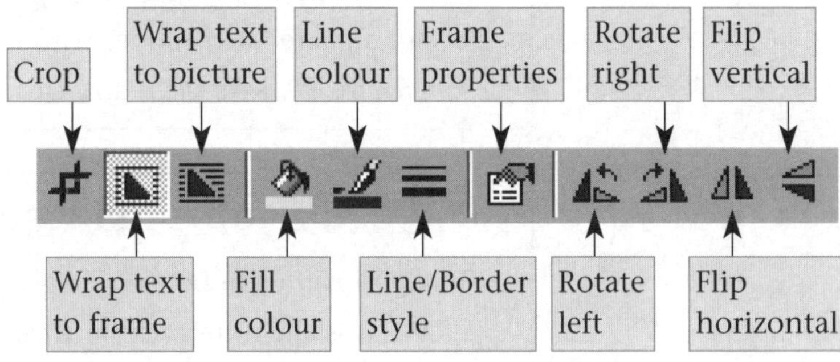

Figure 10.1 Object toolbar for clip art

Hint:

Cropping can be applied to clip art and photographic images.

Method

1 Open a new blank publication – A4 portrait. You will not need to save this file.
2 Insert any clip art image and click on it to select. The Object toolbar appears (Figure 10.1).
3 Click on the **Crop** tool and position it over a side handle – it changes to the crop symbol. Drag this slightly towards the middle of the image and note the effect.

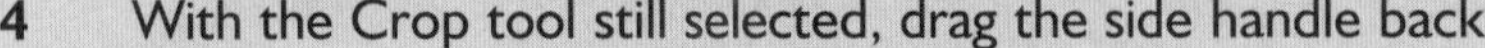

4 With the Crop tool still selected, drag the side handle back.
5 Experiment using the other clip art handles with the Crop tool.

Task 10.2 Rotate and flip an object

Rotating enables you to turn an image, and most other objects, around in a circular direction. Flipping an object turns it over giving you a mirror image. Watch the effect with each tool as you use it.

Method

1. Click on the image to select it.
2. Click on the **Rotate left** tool and repeat 3 more times.
3. Do the same with the **Rotate right** tool.
4. Click on **Flip horizontal** and repeat.
5. Do the same with **Flip vertical**.
6. Click on the **Custom rotate** button on the Standard toolbar  and key in a specific angle, e.g. 45 (Figure 10.2).

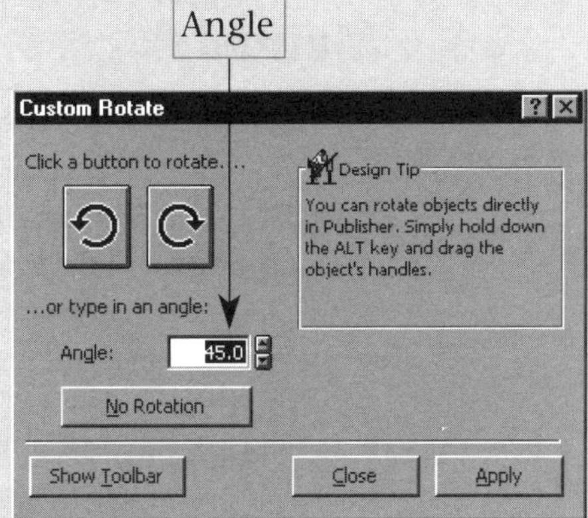

Figure 10.2 Custom rotate

You have already used the other tools you need for clip art but experiment with them now. All of the above tools can also be used with photographic images.

Hint:

From time to time you may be prompted to save this file as you work – click on **No**.

Information: Shape tools

On the toolbox on the left of the screen are several shape tools (Figure 10.3).

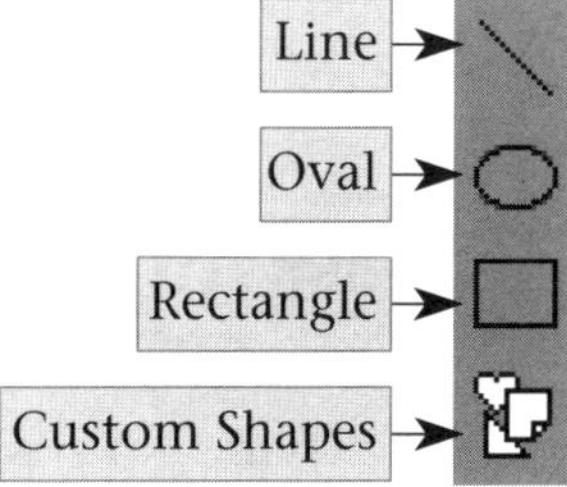

Figure 10.3 Shape tools

Task 10.3 Draw and manipulate lines

You will already be familiar with several of the tools on the toolbar that appears for lines (Figure 10.4).

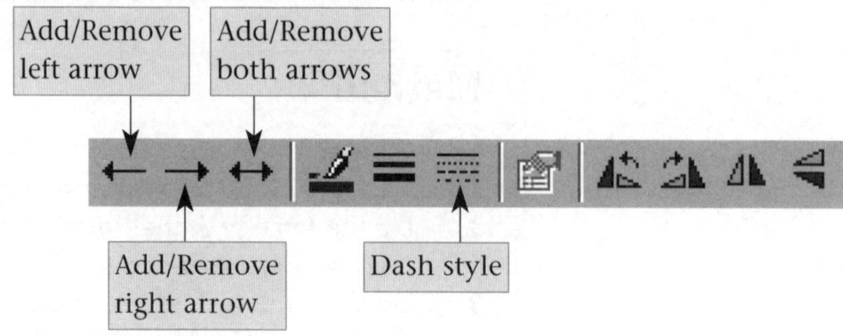

Figure 10.4 Object toolbar for lines

Method

1 Select the **Line** tool and press and drag the mouse to draw a line.
2 Repeat this several times.
3 Hold the Shift key and draw a line – this ensures the line is completely horizontal, vertical or at a 45° angle, dependant upon the direction you drag the end to as you draw.
4 Select a line and click on each of the tools in Figure 10.4 and see the effect.
5 Click on the **Line/Border style** button and choose **More styles**.
6 Choose a line weight of **2 points** and click **OK.**
7 **To resize a line** drag one of the handles.
8 **To move a line** first select it, then position the mouse over the line itself for the **Move** symbol to appear, before dragging to move it.
9 With a line selected, try the **Custom rotate** button 

Hint:

You may need to zoom in to see the effect of the arrows.

Information

Diagonal lines may look jagged but this is because the screen is composed of little dots and this is the only way it can display them. When they print they will be straight. This may also apply to other objects at times.

Task 10.4 Draw and manipulate ovals

The **Oval** tool is not only used for drawing ovals but perfect circles as well. You have already used all the tools on the toolbar for Ovals, which is the same for Rectangles and Custom Shapes – see below.

Figure 10.5 Object toolbar for Oval, Rectangle and Custom Shapes tools

Method

1. Click on the **Oval** tool and press and drag the mouse to draw an oval. Do this several times.
2. With an oval selected, try all the Object toolbar tools above.
3. Click on the **Line/Border style** button and choose **More styles**.
4. Choose a line weight of **4 points** and click **OK.**
5. **To resize an oval** – drag one of the handles.
6. **To move an oval** – first select it, then position the mouse over the shape for the Move symbol to appear before dragging to move it.
7. **To draw a perfect circle** – select the **Oval** tool and hold the Shift key down whilst drawing the shape. This should give you a perfect circle.

Remember:

Holding the Shift key down as you draw a shape gives you a perfect square, circle or custom shape.

Task 10.5 Use fill effects (patterns)

As well as applying fill colours, you can also use fill effects such as patterns.

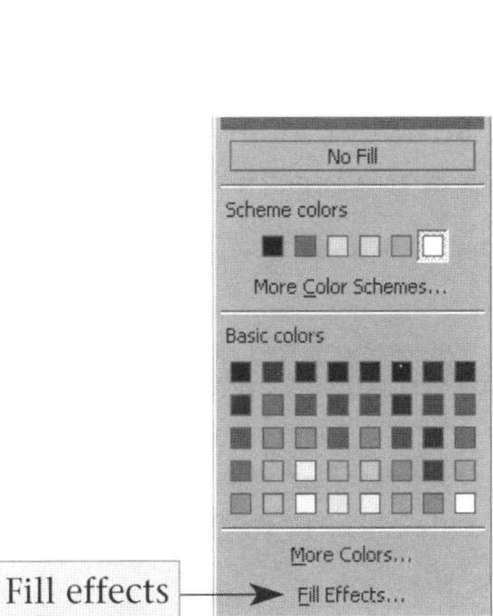

Figure 10.6 Fill effects

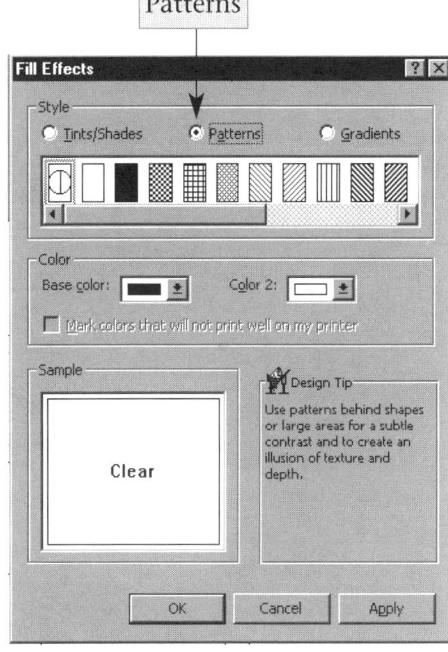

Figure 10.7 Patterns

Method

1. Click on one of the ovals you have drawn and click on the **Fill Color** button.
2. Click on **Fill Effects** (Figure 10.6).
3. Click on **Patterns** (Figure 10.7) and choose one of the patterns.
4. Click **OK**.
5. Repeat this using a different pattern.

Task 10.6 Draw and manipulate rectangles (boxes)

The **Rectangle**, or **Box**, tool is used for drawing rectangles or boxes, and also for perfect squares. The Object toolbar for rectangles can be seen in Figure 10.5.

Method

1 Select the **Rectangle** tool and press and drag the mouse to draw a rectangle. Do this several times.
2 With a rectangle selected, try all the Object toolbar tools as seen in Figure 10.5.
3 **To resize a rectangle** – drag one of the handles.
4 **To move a rectangle** – first select it, then position the mouse over the shape for the Move symbol to appear before dragging to move it.
5 **To draw a perfect square** – select the **Rectangle** tool and hold the Shift key down whilst drawing the shape. This should give you a perfect square
6 Now try the **Custom rotate** button

Remember:

The Rectangle tool is often called the **Box** tool.

Task 10.7 Draw and manipulate custom shapes

The **Custom Shapes** tool gives you a variety of different shapes to choose from. The Object toolbar for Custom Shapes can be see in Figure 10.5.

Method

1 Select the **Custom Shapes** tool and click on a shape to select one.
2 Press and drag the mouse to draw a shape. Do this several times selecting different shapes.
3 With a shape selected, try all the Object toolbar tools as seen in Figure 10.5.
4 **To resize a shape** – drag one of the handles.
5 **To move a shape** – first select it, then position the mouse over the shape for the Move symbol to appear before dragging to move it.
6 **To draw a perfect shape keeping original proportions** – select the **Custom Shape** tool and choose a shape. Hold the Shift key down whilst drawing the shape.
7 Now try the **Custom rotate** button .

Information

Copying objects

Copying objects is the same process as you used in the last section. Any object can be copied and pasted by clicking on it to select, clicking on **Copy** and then **Paste**. Try this now.

Figure 10.8 Cut, copy and paste

Deleting objects

Any object can be deleted by clicking on it to select and pressing **Delete** on the keyboard. Delete all the objects on the page.

Task 10.8 Change an object to a specific size

You have previously resized objects but these can be changed to a specific size.

Method

1 Draw a rectangle and select **Size and Position** from the **Format** menu.

2 Key in **4** in the box alongside **Width** and **6** alongside **Height** (Figure 10.9).

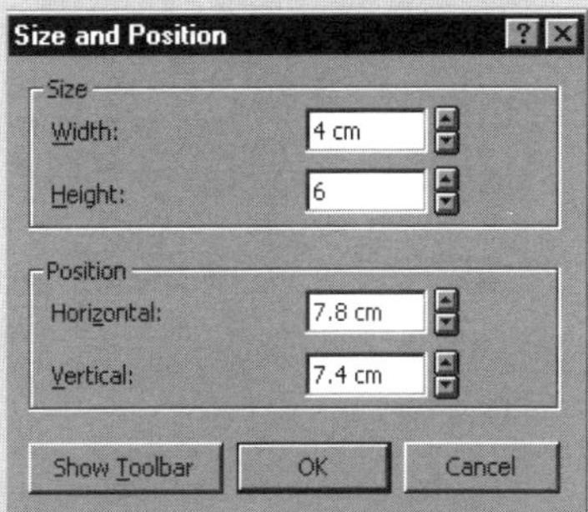

Figure 10.9 Size

3 Click **OK**.

4 Try this again using different measurements. If you use the same measurements for both height and width, you will achieve a perfect square.

5 Try this process on an oval, a custom shape and a horizontal line.

6 Create a text frame and key in your name and try it once more.

7 Delete all objects.

Task 10.9 Place text inside a graphic box

You have already added a border or line around a text frame and filled it. Sometimes you may be required to create a box (or rectangle) and then place a text frame inside (on top of it), effectively giving you two layers.

Method

1. Open a new blank publication and draw a rectangle. Fill it with a pale colour.
2. Create a text frame on top of the rectangle and key in your name. Notice how the text frame is white. This is sometimes the result you require and can look effective especially when you add a border around the text frame.
3. Change the fill (or background) of the text frame to **No fill**.
4. Save the publication as **Layers** into the **Tasks** folder.

Information: Layers

When you are working with layers, you have to imagine one object on top of the other. By selecting a layer you can **Bring it to the front** or **Send it to the back**. In this way you can arrange the layers as you wish.

Task 10.10 Work with layers

Method

1. Click on the text frame to select it and then click on **Send to Back** button on the Formatting toolbar. You cannot now see it although the handles are shown.

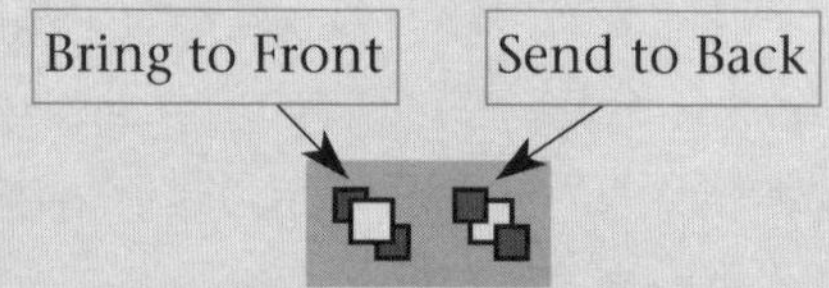

Figure 10.10 Layers buttons

2. Click on **Bring to Front**.
3. Click on the coloured box and then click on **Bring to Front**.
4. Delete all objects.

Try this now with other objects. Draw a box with a fill. Draw a custom shape on top of it and then place a clip art image on top. Experiment with the Layers buttons until you are happy with the way they work.

Hint:

Sometimes if layers go 'wrong' you can move each object aside and then reassemble them in the order you require.

Information: Adding a border to a column

You may be asked to add a border to a column. If it is just a border with No fill, you simply draw a box on the column boundary and ensure it has No fill.

Task 10.11 Add a border to a column

Method

1. Open a new blank publication if necessary and set up two columns.
2. Select the Rectangle tool and draw a box from the top left corner of the first column across to the bottom right-hand corner of the same column. Ensure the fill is set to **No fill.**
3. Repeat for the second column.
4. Draw a text frame across the first column and key in your name and address.
5. Ensure the text frame fill is set to **No fill** or the border may be hidden. You may also need to use **Send to Back**.
6. Repeat inside the second column.

Information: Image resolution

You have previously seen how some shapes appear to be jagged because of the way the screen has to display them as a series of dots. This is the screen resolution.

Resolution also applies to photographic and scanned images which are saved as bitmap images either directly from a digital camera or a scanner. Bitmap images are saved with file extensions like bear.bmp or bear.jpg. These are composed of a grid of dots. The larger the number of dots, the higher the resolution. This in turn gives a better quality image and shows more detail. A low resolution image would be composed of fewer dots and would show less detail. If you enlarge a bitmap image the dots get bigger and the quality of the image deteriorates, becoming fuzzy and showing less detail, as you can see in Figure 10.11 below.

Figure 10.11 Resolution

Hint:

A file extension is the second part of a filename preceded by a dot, e.g. bear.jpg. The file extension indicates the file type, e.g. a Word file might be letter.doc. Depending on your setup you might not see these in the normal course of your work.

→ Practise your skills 1

1. Open a new blank publication – A4 landscape, margins of 2 cm, two columns with a gutter of 2 cm. (Use ruler guides for the gutter.)
2. Draw a border around each column and fill each with a pale colour.
3. Save as **Animal Hotel** into the **Skills Practice** folder.
4. Create a text box within the left column leaving a space around the edge so that the background colour shows and key in the following text. **Hint:** Use Bring to Front and Send to Back if layers 'disappear'.

   Wheatsheaf Animal Hotel
   Crofthill
   Berkshire
   For short and long stay
   Homely environment
   Individual pens
   Quarantine
   Special diets catered for
   Inspection visits welcome
5. Ensure the fill colour of the text frame is set to white and add a border.
6. Centre the text, format as you wish and space it out to fill the frame, keeping the address in single spacing.
7. Draw a circle and resize it to 4 cm in width and height.
8. Fill the circle with a pattern and a no border style (choose None).
9. Position in the top left corner of the right-hand column.
10. Copy the circle and place it in the bottom right corner of the same column.
11. Create a box and resize it to 3 cm square. Fill with a pale colour. Change the border line weight to 2 pt.
12. Position it in the top right corner of the right-hand column.
13. Rotate it to an angle of 45° to form a diamond shape.
14. Copy and paste it, moving the copy to the bottom left of the same column.
15. Insert a clip art image of a cat and one of a dog, resizing them to fit one in a circle and the other in a diamond.
16. Copy the images and flip the copy horizontally in each case.
17. Position the copies in the empty shapes.
18. Create a text frame and resize it to 8 × 1.5 cm, positioning it in the middle of the right-hand column.
19. Ensure the fill is white and add a border.
20. Key in **Competitive rates**.
21. Centre the text, increase the font size to 24 and choose a font.
22. Proofread, checking text and images, and ensuring that all objects are fully visible.
23. Save, print and close.

→ Check your knowledge

1. What does cropping mean?
2. Give two ways of rotating an object.
3. What does flip mean?
4. How can you change an object to a specific size?
5. How does the resolution of a bitmap image affect its quality and level of detail?

Consolidation 3

1 Make a note of the available memory (RAM) and storage space on your computer system.

2 Write down one use of a scanner.

3 Create a new folder and call it **Nursery**.

4 Create a new blank publication with the following specification:

Orientation	Portrait
Left Margin	2 cm (0.75″)
Right Margin	2 cm (0.75″)
Top Margin	2 cm (0.75″)
Bottom Margin	2 cm (0.75″)
Columns	2
Gutter	0.5 cm (0.25″) (this is the default)

5 Save the publication as **Summer Picnic** into the new folder.

6 Place a border round each column. (Draw a rectangle or box.)

7 Draw a box across the top of the margin stretching from left to right margin and fill it with a pale colour. Make the box 4 cm (1.5″) in height.

8 Insert the following text into this box. (Draw a text frame.)
Waterford Nursery
Essex Way
Watchingdon

9 Centre the text and change it to a suitable size. Ensure the background colour shows through (apply No fill to the text frame).

10 Find a suitable picture of a child and insert it at the bottom of the first column.

11 Copy the image and move the copy to the top of the second column, enlarging it to fill up approximately half of the column.

12 Flip this second image horizontally.

13 Create a text frame in the first column and key in the following:
Summer Picnic
Saturday August 17th
From 12.30 pm
Victoria Park
By the paddling pool

14 Apply superscript to the **th** of the date.

15 Draw a box with a border and size it to 4 cm square.

16 This box is to be positioned below the words **Summer Picnic** so leave line spacing after the heading of 120 points. (You can also press Enter to create space.)

17 Centre the text and format as you wish, applying suitable line spacing.

18 Insert a clip art image of a picnic or food in the box in the left column, sizing it to fit.

19 Create a text frame in the second column and key in the following:
All the family welcome
Parents
Grandparents
Brothers and sisters
Ask Joy for more details

20 Centre and format the text as you wish choosing suitable line spacing.

21 Proofread, checking text and images, and ensuring that all objects are fully visible.

22 Add your name in a text frame just below the bottom margin on the left and the date in a separate text frame on the right.

23 Save, print and close.

Section 11 Print and file output considerations

You will learn to

- Understand reasons for:
  - Previewing before printing
  - Printing draft copies
- Print multiple copies
- Print to file

In this section will find out about various print options, such as printing drafts and changing printer resolution, and why you might do that. You will also learn how publications may be prepared for commercial printing.

Information

Previewing before printing

Some computer applications give you the chance to preview your work to check it before you print, to see what it will look like and whether the layout is as required. If you have used Excel for example, you may have used its preview facility. Publisher is a **WYSIWYG** program, which stands for **W**hat **Y**ou **S**ee **I**s **W**hat **Y**ou **G**et. In other words, what you see on the screen is what you see on your printout, so you are actually previewing your work all the time. You can, however, view your page in **Whole Page** view, which gives you the opportunity to see how the complete page will look. It is important to check your work before you print because you can waste printouts, and therefore ink or toner, if something is wrong. If you should be using a colour printer then this would be particularly expensive. You may also be sending your publication to a commercial printing company and you therefore must make sure it is correct to avoid expensive reprinting.

Draft copies and resolution

When printing, it is possible with most printers to print a draft or a lower resolution copy of a publication. This would save ink or toner. In the previous section you learnt about resolution of images. Similarly with printouts, you can usually change the resolution. The higher the resolution, the more dots are used and therefore the level of detail is better. In the examples below, there are three different resolutions – 1200 dpi (dots per inch, i.e. per square inch), 600 dpi and 300 dpi.

1200 dpi

600 dpi

300 dpi

Figure 11.1 Print resolution

→

If you look at the 1200 dpi version, you can see two shades of grey on the wings. On the 600 dpi version you can still see the two shades of grey but the dots are more visible because they are spaced further apart. On the 300 dpi version the shades are barely visible and altogether not so clear and crisp.

With the printer featured in Figure 11.2, resolution is found in Advanced printing options. All printers are different and you will have to look at your own printer manual or ask your tutor how to achieve this. Select **Print** from the **File** menu for print options. Do this now and compare your own printouts of a publication containing images.

It is always a good idea to give a draft copy of your work to someone else to check as it is easy to miss your own mistakes. A fresh eye is always useful in spotting errors and offering an opinion or suggestion on layout.

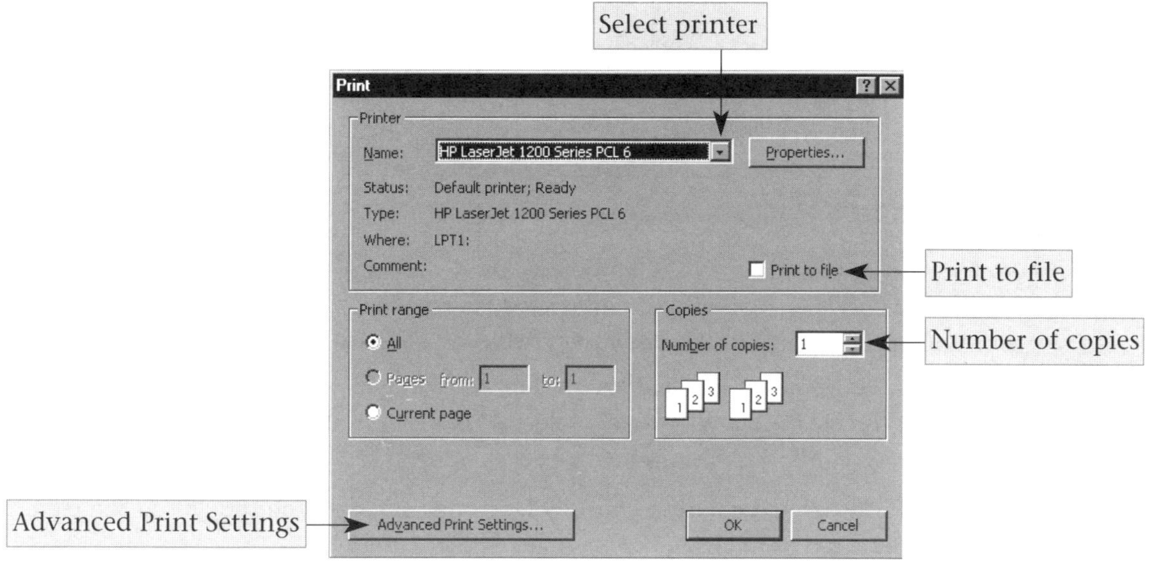

Figure 11.2 Print options

Information: Print multiple copies

It is possible to print more than one copy of a publication at a time.

Task 11.1 Print multiple copies

Method

1. With any publication open, select **Print** from the **File** menu.
2. Key in **2** in the **Number of copies:** box (Figure 11.2).
3. Click **OK**.

Information: Print to file

You may be asked to print a publication into a file that you can take to a commercial print company. You might also do this to print at a later stage although you can always print a saved file later. When you do this you will be prompted for a filename and a location for your file.

Task 11.2 Print to file

Method

1 With any publication open, select **Print** from the **File** menu.
2 Click in the box **Print to file** (Figure 11.2 above) and click **OK**.

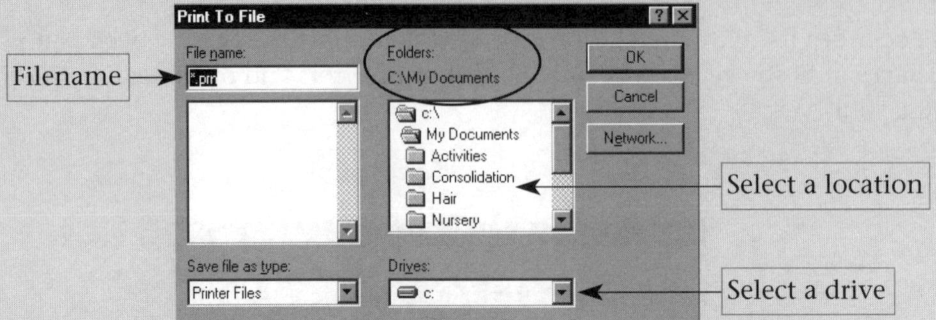

Figure 11.3 Print to file

3 Click in the **File name:** box (Figure 11.3) and delete the * (not .prn), keying in the name **Sample**.
4 In the example above the file is printed to C:\My Documents. This is My Documents on the C: drive of a single computer. If you are using a network, it may say N: drive. Check with your tutor.

If you want to print the file into a folder, click on the required folder.
If you want to print the file onto a floppy disk, select A: drive from the drive list.

5 Click **OK**.

If you minimise or close Publisher and check in your My Documents folder, you should see Sample.prn. The file extension .prn indicates it is a print file.

Try this again using a different filename.

There are other methods of preparing files for commercial printing.

→ Practise your skills 1

1 Open any publication and print 2 copies of the publication.
2 Print a draft copy at a lower resolution. Write on your printout indicating it is a draft.
3 Print the publication to file giving it a suitable name. Check it appears as a .prn file in My Documents or wherever you printed it to. Show this to your tutor.

→ Check your knowledge

1 Why is it important to check a publication is correct before printing?
2 What does dpi mean?
3 What does print to file mean and why might you do it?
4 Why is it important to produce a draft copy of your work for someone else to check before final printing?
5 What is a draft copy?

Practice assignments

Practice assignment 1

Read all instructions carefully before starting work and check with your assessor, if necessary, that you have fully understood them.

Scenario
You have been asked to produce a leaflet for The Circle, a health and fitness club, to promote their facilities. (See next page).

Task

1 Write down the amount of available memory (RAM) and storage.

2 Write down one advantage of scanning text for using in desktop publishing.

3 Create a folder called **The Circle**.

4 Load Publisher and create a new publication and save it as **Open Day** into the new folder.

5 Set up a new A4 page to the following specifications:

Orientation	Portrait
Left Margin	2 cm (0.75″)
Right Margin	2 cm (0.75″)
Top Margin	2 cm (0.75″)
Bottom Margin	2 cm (0.75″)
Columns	2
Gutter	0.5 cm (0.25″) (this is the default)

6 Place a border around each column.

7 Draw a box just below the top margin that stretches from left to right margin, with a pale colour fill and a border. Resize it to a height of 4 cm.

8 Insert the following text into this box with a No fill text frame:
THE CIRCLE
Open Day

9 Format it as follows:
- Centre and bold
- Select a suitable font, size 28

10 Draw a circle with a width and height of 1.5 cm, a pattern fill and no border. Position it in the bottom left corner of the first column. Copy and paste it into the bottom right corner of the second column.

11 Type the text into the first column as shown in Column 1 below and format as follows:

- Align the text to the right
- Choose a suitable font, size 20
- Underline **All for free**!
- Put the **th** of the date into superscript.

12 Draw a box 4 cm square and position as shown in Column 1 below.

13 Copy the box in Column 1 and paste it into Column 2, rotating it by 45°.

14 Enter the text shown in Column 2 and format as follows:
- Same font as used in Column 1, size 20
- Align to the left.

15 Add your name at the foot of the page on the left.

16 Add the text **Draft printout** at the foot of the page on the right.

17 Save the file and print a draft copy at a low resolution. Close the file.

18 Check the draft copy and note on it any necessary amendments.

19 Re-open the file and make the amendments.

20 Insert suitable clip art into the two boxes.

21 Move text **Pilates** in front of **Aerobics**

22 Amend the text at the foot of the page to read **Final Printout**.

23 Save as **Open Day 2**.

24 Print the publication.

25 Print the publication to file with the name **Circle.prn**.

Hand in
Your answers to No 1 and 2.
Both printouts.

Show your tutor your .prn file and your new folder.

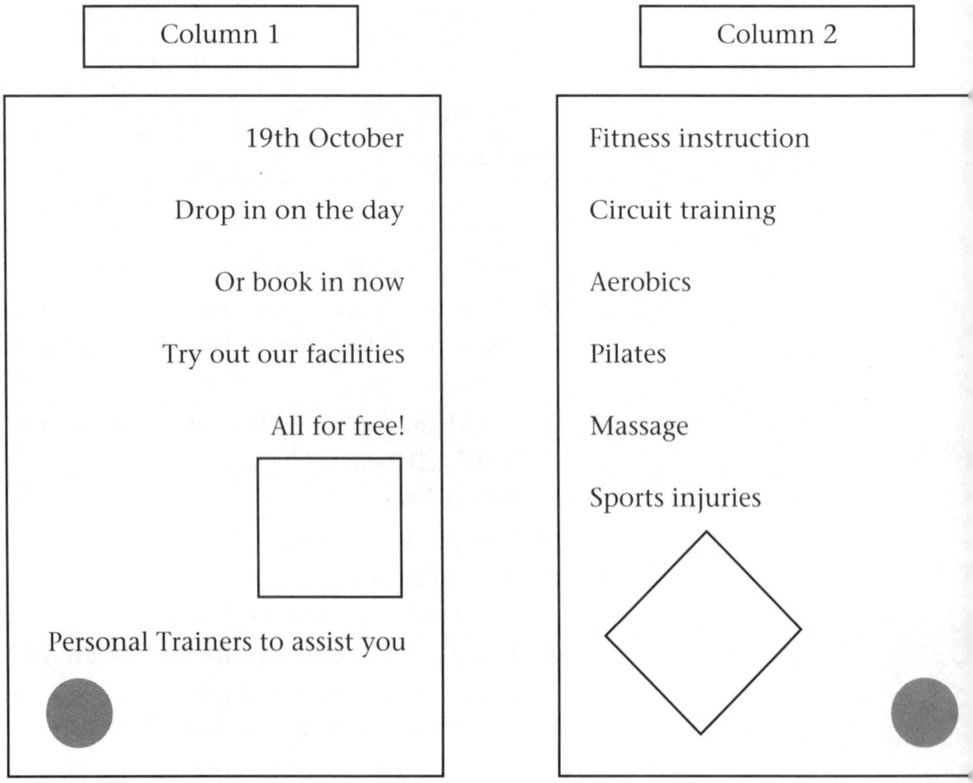

Column 1	Column 2
19th October	Fitness instruction
Drop in on the day	Circuit training
Or book in now	Aerobics
Try out our facilities	Pilates
All for free!	Massage
	Sports injuries
Personal Trainers to assist you	

Practice assignment 2

Read all instructions carefully before starting work and check with your assessor, if necessary, that you have fully understood them.

Scenario
You work for a local furniture showroom and there is a sale coming up. You have been asked to produce a leaflet for this special promotion and have been given a rough sketch. (See next page.)

Task

1 Write down two uses of a scanner for desktop publishing.

2 Write down the difference between a draft and final printout in terms of resolution and quality.

3 Create a folder called **Furniture**.

4 Load Publisher and create a new publication and save it as **Sales Leaflet** into the new folder.

5 Set up a new A4 page to the following specifications:

Orientation	Landscape
Left Margin	2.5 cm (1″)
Right Margin	2.5 cm (1″)
Top Margin	2.5 cm (1″)
Bottom Margin	2.5 cm (1″)
Columns	3
Gutter	0.5 cm (0.25″)

6 Create a box at the top stretching from left to right margins with a height of 3.5 cm and a light grey fill.

7 Key in the text as shown in this space with a No fill text frame and format as follows:
- Centre and embolden
- Arial size 24 or another sans serif font if this is not available
- Put the last line into italics
- Put the **st** of the date into superscript.

8 Draw a box across the bottom of the page with a height of 1.5 cm and light grey fill.

9 Key in the text in this box with a No fill text frame as shown using the same font and format as follows:
- Size 24
- Centred
- Very loose character spacing.

10 Key in the text in each column, leaving a line space after each column heading.

11 Change all text to the same font as used for the main heading.

12 Change the column headings to size 24 and underline them

13 Change the remaining text to size 20.

14 Draw a horizontal line at the bottom of the middle column with a width of 6 cm and an arrow head at each end.

15 Insert suitable clip art into each column where indicated on the sketch.

16 Add your name and the date at the foot of the page on the left.

17 On the right add a label reading **First printout**.

18 Save the file and print a draft copy at a low resolution. Close the file.

19 Check the draft copy and indicate any necessary amendments.

20 Re-open the file and make any necessary changes.

21 Flip each of the clip art images horizontally.

22 In the first column move **Lamps** in front of **Coffee Tables**.

23 In the third column move **Bedding** in front of **Wardrobes**.

24 Amend the text at the foot of the page to read **Final Printout**.

25 Save as Sales Leaflet 2 and print.

26 Print the publication to file with the name Leaflet.prn.

Hand in

Your answers to No 1 and 2.

Both printouts.

Show your tutor your .prn file and your new folder.

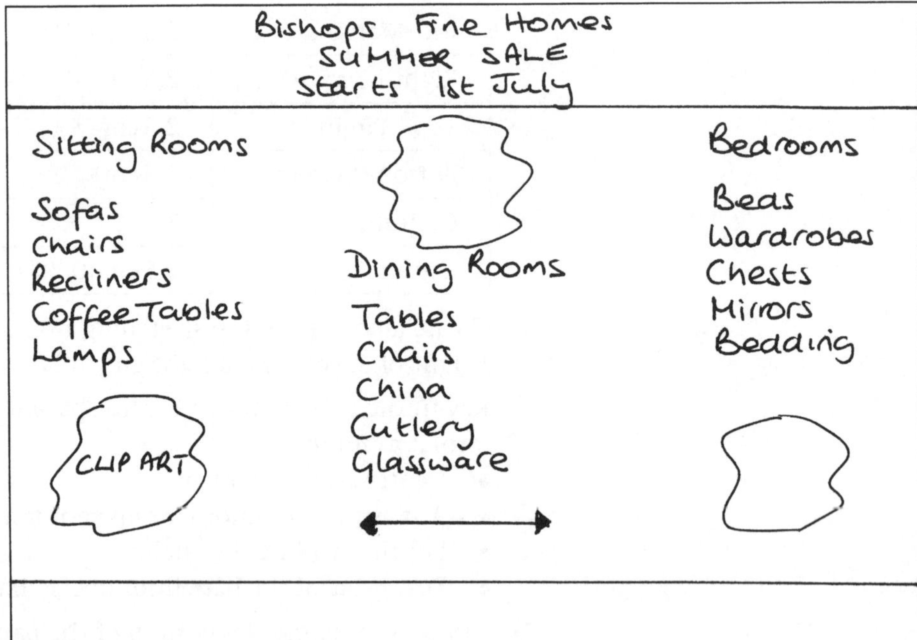

Has a Tutor seen your blue RECORD OF PROGRESS card recently?

IF NOT ASK A TUTOR TO CHECK YOUR PROGRESS NOW

Solutions

Section 1 Getting started

Practise your skills 1

Causeway Motors

Full Servicing Facilities

MOT Testing Station

Repairs to all makes of cars

Breakdown and Recovery Service

The Causeway
Bishopsford

Practise your skills 2

SUMMER ACTIVITIES

FOR

5–12 YEAR OLDS

Throughout August

at

Kingsland School

A range of activities:

Swimming
Tennis
Football
Badminton
Team Games
Trampolining
Gymnastics

Pick up an application form from reception now

Check your knowledge

1 Portrait is tall.
2 The onscreen version of a file.
3 A publication.
4 For temporarily placing objects whilst deciding where to position them on the page.
5 Select Print Setup from the File menu and choose required size.

Section 2 Editing text

Practise your skills 1

Causeway Motor Company

Full Servicing Facilities

MOT Testing Station

Speedy repairs to all makes of cars

24 Hour Breakdown and Recovery

The Causeway
Bishopsford

Practise your skills 2

SUMMER ACTIVITIES

FOR

5–12 YEAR OLDS

Throughout August

at

Kingsland Junior School

A range of fully supervised activities:

Swimming
Tennis
Football
Badminton
Team Games
Athletics
Gymnastics

Pick up a leaflet from reception now

Check your knowledge

1. Save your work every ten minutes in case a system error or power failure occurs. You would then only lose work up to your last save.
2. The spellcheck does not spot words that are correctly spelt but used in the wrong context, e.g. Are ewe coming with me? It does not check for sense or meaning.
3. Open an existing publication.
4. Save a publication.
5. When saving a file for the first time you must name it. Subsequently using Save will save an amended file replacing the original. Save As allows you to give a file a new name or save to a new location.

Section 3 Formatting text

Practise your skills 1

Causeway Motor Company

Full Servicing Facilities

MOT Testing Station

Speedy repairs to all makes of cars

24 Hour Breakdown and Recovery

The Causeway
Bishopsford

Practise your skills 2

SUMMER ACTIVITIES

FOR

5-12 YEAR OLDS

Throughout August

at

Kingsland Junior School

A range of fully supervised activities:

Swimming
Tennis
Football
Badminton
Team Games
Athletics
Gymnastics

Pick up a leaflet from reception now

Check your knowledge

1 Double click on the word. (Or you can drag to highlight it.)

2 Serifs are little strokes at the ends of characters which sans serif characters do not have (sans means without).

3 Text in overflow.

4 When text cannot fit into a frame it is held in the overflow area.

5 Left justified text – each line starts at the left margin of the text frame but the right-hand side is ragged. Right justified – each line ends at the right margin but the left is ragged. Centred – each line is centred between the left and right-hand margins. Fully justified – each line starts at the left and ends exactly at the right-hand margin.

Consolidation 1

Mobile Hairdresser

Experienced hairdresser will visit you in your own home

Cuts
Blow drys
Tints
Perms

Lady and gentleman customers welcome.

Competitive rates
20% reduction for your first appointment

Telephone Franki now on 0927324128

Section 4 Working with images

Practise your skills 1

Causeway Motor Company

Full Servicing Facilities

MOT Testing Station

Speedy repairs to all makes of cars

24 Hour Breakdown and Recovery

The Causeway
Bishopsford

Practise your skills 2

SUMMER ACTIVITIES

FOR

5-12 YEAR OLDS

Throughout August

at

Kingsland Junior School

A range of fully supervised activities:

Swimming
Tennis
Football
Badminton
Team Games
Athletics
Gymnastics

Pick up a leaflet from reception now

Check your knowledge

1 Position pointer over a corner handle – pointer changes to a resize handle – and drag inwards or outwards.

2 Make sure you use a corner handle.

3 Hold down the Alt key and use the arrow keys on the keyboard.

4 If you want text to wrap around an image apply text wrap around objects. If not, ensure that option is deselected.

5 Click on the text frame. Click on Text Frame Properties button or select Text Frame Properties from the Format menu. Click on Text wrap around objects check box. This is usually on by default.

Section 5 Working with folders

Check your knowledge

1 Nothing – they mean the same thing.

2 To store related files together so they can be found easily.

3 Give it a name that relates to its contents.

4 To make a backup copy in case something happens to the original, or if you want to take the file elsewhere.

5 That the disk drive light has gone out.

Section 6 Page layout

Practise your skills 1

QUARRYFIELDS COLLEGE

City & Guilds

e-Quals

Level 1

Starting next month

For information call in now

Level 2 also available

IT Principles
Word Processing
Spreadsheets
Databases
Using the Internet
Presentation Graphics
E-Mail
Desktop Publishing

Practise your skills 2

QUARRYFIELDS COLLEGE

Courses for the Autumn

Enrolling NOW

Call in any time between

9 am and 7 pm

Vocational Courses

Leisure Courses

VOCATIONAL COURSES

Information Technology
Business
Health and Social Care
Media Studies
Catering
And many more ...

LEISURE COURSES

Art
Cookery
Sports
Yoga
Flower Arranging
And many more ...

Check your knowledge

1 A4 portrait.

2 A3 is twice the size of A4. A4 is twice the size of A5. A5 is twice the size of A6.

3 The gap between two columns.

4 To give interest to the page, to make it easier to read, to split it into sections or to divide the page for the creation of folding leaflets.

5 When 2 spaces are left between lines rather than the normal one.

Consolidation 2

Pepe's Pizza Palace

Pizzas

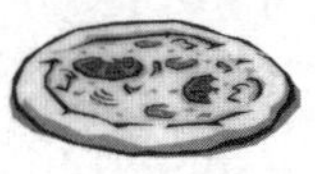

Original Cheese
Pepperoni
Spicy Chilli
Vegetarian
Chicken Supreme
Tropical Surpise
Sausage and Bacon

Extras

13 Market Place
Pitford
Tel 0987 736736

Take-away Menu

Garlic Bread
Potato Wedges
French Fries
Soft drinks
Banoffee Pie

Section 7 Further formatting

Practise your skills 1

Practise your skills 2

Check your knowledge

1. It means to adjust the spacing between characters to make them closer together or further apart.
2. Subscript characters are small characters that appear just below the characters around it, e.g. H_20. Superscript characters are raised just above, e.g. 10°C.
3. It means the fill colour applied to a text frame or an object, such as clip art, is transparent.

4 It wraps text around an object following its shape.
5 Highlight it and select **Font** from the **Format** menu. Click on the **All caps** option.

Section 8 The DTP environment

Practise your skills 1

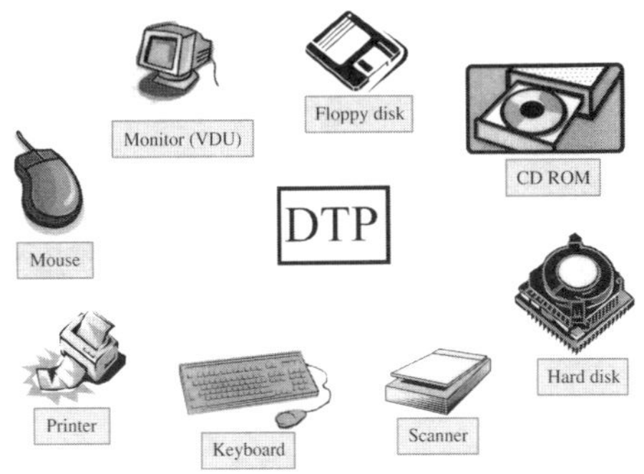

Check your knowledge

1 To scan images and text.
2 Either it enables you to scan and insert any image into your work or it scans your text into a file. You can then insert into a publication and edit and format, saving you time in having to recreate it.
3 Random Access Memory.
4 To ensure there is sufficient memory to be able to hold your work as you are creating it and to make sure there is enough space to save your completed work.
5 Text editing, word processing and graphics software.

Section 9 Further page layout and copy and paste

Practise your skills 1

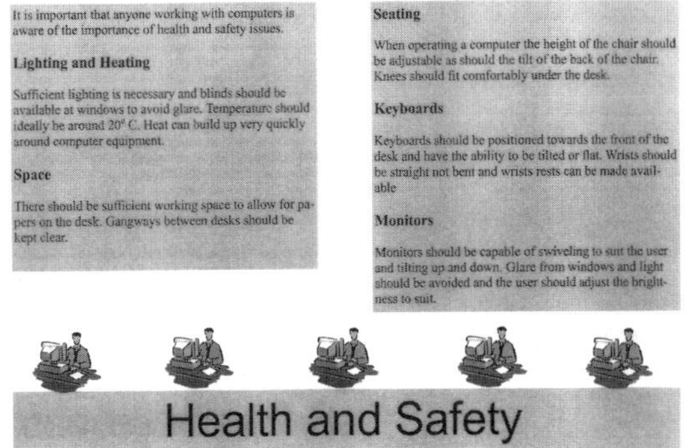

It is important that anyone working with computers is aware of the importance of health and safety issues.

Lighting and Heating

Sufficient lighting is necessary and blinds should be available at windows to avoid glare. Temperature should ideally be around 20° C. Heat can build up very quickly around computer equipment.

Space

There should be sufficient working space to allow for papers on the desk. Gangways between desks should be kept clear.

Seating

When operating a computer the height of the chair should be adjustable as should the tilt of the back of the chair. Knees should fit comfortably under the desk.

Keyboards

Keyboards should be positioned towards the front of the desk and have the ability to be tilted or flat. Wrists should be straight not bent and wrists rests can be made available

Monitors

Monitors should be capable of swiveling to suit the user and tilting up and down. Glare from windows and light should be avoided and the user should adjust the brightness to suit.

Health and Safety

Check your knowledge

1 An area of memory where an object or text is held whilst in the process of pasting or moving it elsewhere.
2 Copy and paste leaves the original in place and produces another copy, whereas cut and paste takes out the original and allows you to paste it elsewhere.
3 Ruler guides.

Section 10 Manipulating graphic objects

Practise your skills 1

Check your knowledge

1 It means to cover over part of an image so it does not show.

2 Select an object and either click on Rotate left or Rotate right, or use Custom rotate.

3 It flips over an object to give a mirror image.

4 Select the object and choose Size and Position from the Format menu. Key in required measurements.

5 As a bitmap image is made up of a grid of dots, the more dots there are, the higher the resolution is and the better the quality. Higher quality gives a higher level of detail.

Consolidation 3

Section 11 Print and file output considerations

Check your knowledge

1 You waste printouts if something is wrong. Wasted colour printouts are particularly expensive. If you are using a commercial printing company you must avoid expensive reprinting.

2 Dots per inch (dots per square inch).

3 It means to print into a file that you can take to a commercial print company or perhaps to print later.

4 Because it is easy to miss your own mistakes. A fresh eye is always useful in spotting errors and also offering an opinion or suggestion on layout.

5 A printout made at a lower resolution, i.e. with a lower dpi.

Practice assignments

Practice assignment 1

2 It scans the text into a text file that can be inserted directly into a publication where it can be edited and formatted,

or

It saves time in having to key it all in.

Practice assignment 2

1 For scanning images to insert into a publication.
For scanning text into a text file that can be inserted into a publication, edited and formatted.

2 A draft printout is at a lower resolution than a final printout. The higher the resolution, the more dots are used and therefore the level of detail is better.

Outcomes matching guide

Outcome 1 Use the DTP system environment		
Practical activities		
1	Use computer hardware for DTP: Random Access Memory, monitor (VDU), mouse, keyboard, hard disk, floppy disk, CD-ROM, printer	All sections All sections All sections Sections 4, 5 All sections
2	Use the operating system to manage directories/folders and files	Section 5
3	Check the available memory (RAM) and storage space	Section 8
4	Create a new DTP file	All sections
5	Open an existing DTP file	Section 2 onwards
6	Save an edited DTP file without changing its name	All sections except 5
7	Save a DTP file with a new name	Section 2 onwards
Underpinning knowledge		
1	Identify the use of scanners	Section 8
2	Identify the importance of checking the available memory (RAM) and storage space before creating DTP files	Section 8
3	Identify the common types of applications software used for creating elements of a DTP publication: graphics, DTP, text editor, word processor	Section 8
Outcome 2 Set up given page layouts		
Practical activities		
1	Change page margins: top, bottom, right, left	Section 6 onwards
2	Set columns with gutters	Section 6 onwards
3	Use different page sizes A4 A5	Sections 1, 2, 3 onwards Section 3 onwards
4	Change page orientation	Sections 3, 6 onwards
Underpinning knowledge		
1	Identify the common paper sizes: A3, A4, A5, A6	Section 6
2	Identify the reasons for using columns in a page layout	Section 6
3	Identify the difference between landscape and portrait orientation	Section 1

Outcome 3 Manipulate text in a DTP file		
Practical activities		
1	Enter and edit text	Sections 1, 2
2	Select text	Section 3
3	Change the text formats: • font (serif, sans serif), font size, colour, bold, italics, underline • upper and lower case, subscript and superscript • line and character spacing • justification	 Section 3 Section 7 Sections 6, 7 Section 3
4	Move text	Section 9
5	Copy text	Section 9
6	Apply fill styles to a selected area	Section 7
7	Insert, delete and position text	Section 2 onwards
8	Use wrap settings	Section 4
Underpinning knowledge		
1	List types of justification: left justified, right justified, centred, fully justified	Section 3
Outcome 4 Manipulate graphic objects		
Practical activities		
1	Select a graphic object	Sections 4, 10
2	Move a graphic object	Sections 4, 10
3	Copy a graphic object	Sections 9, 10
4	Insert and position a graphic object	Sections 4, 10
5	Delete a graphic object	Sections 4, 10
6	Change the attributes/properties of a graphic object: size, position, shape, border, background	Section 10
7	Draw lines, circles and boxes: line thickness, colour, line style	Section 10
8	Change the attributes/properties of lines, circles and boxes	Section 10
9	Add a box round text	Section 7
10	Place text inside a graphic box	Section 10
11	Apply flip/mirror, scale, rotate and crop to a graphic object	Section 10
Underpinning knowledge		
1	State that resolution defines the level of detail of an image made up of dots	Section 10
2	State that the greater the number of separate dots that make up an image the higher the quality the image is	Section 10

Outcome 5 Produce printed and file outputs		
Practical activities		
1	Use the application preview facility to view and check that output is suitable for printing	Section 11
2	Produce a draft copy for checking before final printing	Section 11
3	Produce final output as instructions: resolution, number of copies	Section 11
4	Save printed output to disk	All sections
Underpinning knowledge		
1	State the importance of checking and correcting output before printing	Section 11
2	State the importance of printing a draft copy for checking by others before final printing	Section 11
3	State that a draft copy is printed at a lower resolution	Section 11
4	State that printed output can be sent to a disk file: • To be printed at a later stage • To be sent for printing to a professional print bureau	Section 11

Quick reference guide

Action	Button	Menu	Keyboard
Arrows	Draw line and click on		
Bring to Front			
Bold	B	Format – Font – Font style	Ctrl + B
Cancel			Esc
Centre align			Ctrl + E
Character spacing		Format – Character spacing	
Close or Exit		File – Close or Exit	Alt + F4
Columns		Arrange – Layout guides	
Copy		Edit – Copy	Ctrl + C
Crop			
Cut		Edit – Cut	Ctrl + X
End of Line			End
Exit or Close		File – Close or Exit	Alt + F4
Fill – colour/ patterns			
Flip/mirror			
Font	Arial	Format – Font – Font	
Font colour	A	Format – Font – Colour	
Font size	12	Format – Font – Size	
Gutter	Accept default using Arrange – Layout guides or create Ruler guides – see Ruler guides		
Insert clip art		Insert – Picture – ClipArt	
Insert Picture		Insert – Picture – from File	
Italics	I	Format – Font	Ctrl + I
Justify			Ctrl + J
Left align			Ctrl + L
Line/Border style			

Line colour			
Line spacing		Format – Line spacing	
Margins		Arrange – Layout guides	
New publication		File – New	Ctrl + N
Open file		File – Open	Ctrl + O
Paper size/ orientation		File – Print Setup	
Paste		Edit – Paste	Ctrl + V
Print		File – Print	Ctrl + P
Print to file		File – Print – click on Print to file	
Redo		Edit – Redo	
Right align			Ctrl + R
Rotate	or		
Ruler guides	Hold shift down, drag from ruler		
Save		File – Save	Ctrl + S
Save As		File – Save As	F12
Select All (in a text frame)		Edit – Select All	Ctrl + A
Send to Back			
Spellcheck		Tools – Spelling	F7
Start of line			Home
Text frame	A		
Text wrap (apply to text frame)			
Underline	U	Format – Font – Underline	Ctrl + U
Undo		Edit – Undo	
Upper case		Format – Font – All caps	
View options	50% – +	View – Zoom	
Zoom	50% – +	View – Zoom	

Select text

To select:	Method
One word	Double click on word (also selects the following space)
Several words	Press and drag the I-beam across several words and release
To deselect	Click anywhere off the text

Right mouse button

Clicking the right mouse button provides menu options depending on what you are doing at the time, e.g. when right clicked in text, you have Cut, Copy, Paste, etc.

Object toolbar for images – most tools applicable to other objects

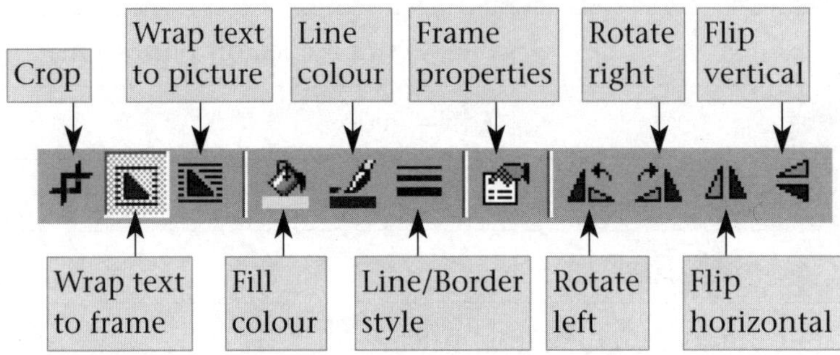